PETS™

Primary Education Thinking Skills Curriculum - 1

Updated Edition

Jody Nichols, Sally Thomson, Margaret Wolfe, and Dodie Merritt

Illustrated by Dodie Merritt

Cover by John Steele

Pieces of Learning
1990 Market Road
Marion IL 62959
www.piecesoflearning.com
CLC0483
ISBN 978-1-937113-03-2
Printed by McNaughton & Gunn, Inc.
Saline MI USA
05/2012

Acknowledgments

The authors of this book would like to thank the administration of Illinois School Districts #47 and #424 for their support of the PETS™ program as well as the many primary teachers in whose classes these materials were field-tested. Also many thanks to our families for their support.

A special thanks to Ryan Arens, Devin Beggs, Jami Biedermann, Travis Brown, Kelly Chrystal, Jessica Doerrfeld, Grainger Greene, Lindsey Hines, Alaine Lecuyer, Felicia Lee, Keith McKenna, Adam McNerney, Mark Meador, Morgan Meredith, Drew Nystrom, Jessica Ocheskey, Josh Osborn, Sarah Pierce, Heidi Quinn, Kierstyn Rauch, Evan Schano, Chris Schroeder, Becca Terdich, Christina Werderitch, Brynn Wolford and Tim Yaguchi for the contribution of their artwork to "Laboratory Limpets" *and* "Sybil's Creatures."

A note to our readers ...

Throughout the text, we alternate between "he" and "she" when referring to the students. Not only does this reinforce an awareness that both boys and girls benefit from this type of programming, but it is also much more reader-friendly than always saying "he/she."

TABLE OF CONTENTS

Primary Education Thinking Skills (PETS™) Introduction . . 5

Dudley the Detective
Convergent / Deductive Thinking 17

Isabel the Inventor
Divergent / Inventive Thinking 63

Sybil the Scientist
Convergent / Analytical Thinking 93

Yolanda the Yarnspinner
Divergent / Creative Thinking 129

Max the Magician
Visual/Spatial Perception 159

Jordan the Judge
Evaluative Thinking 187

Cast of Characters 219

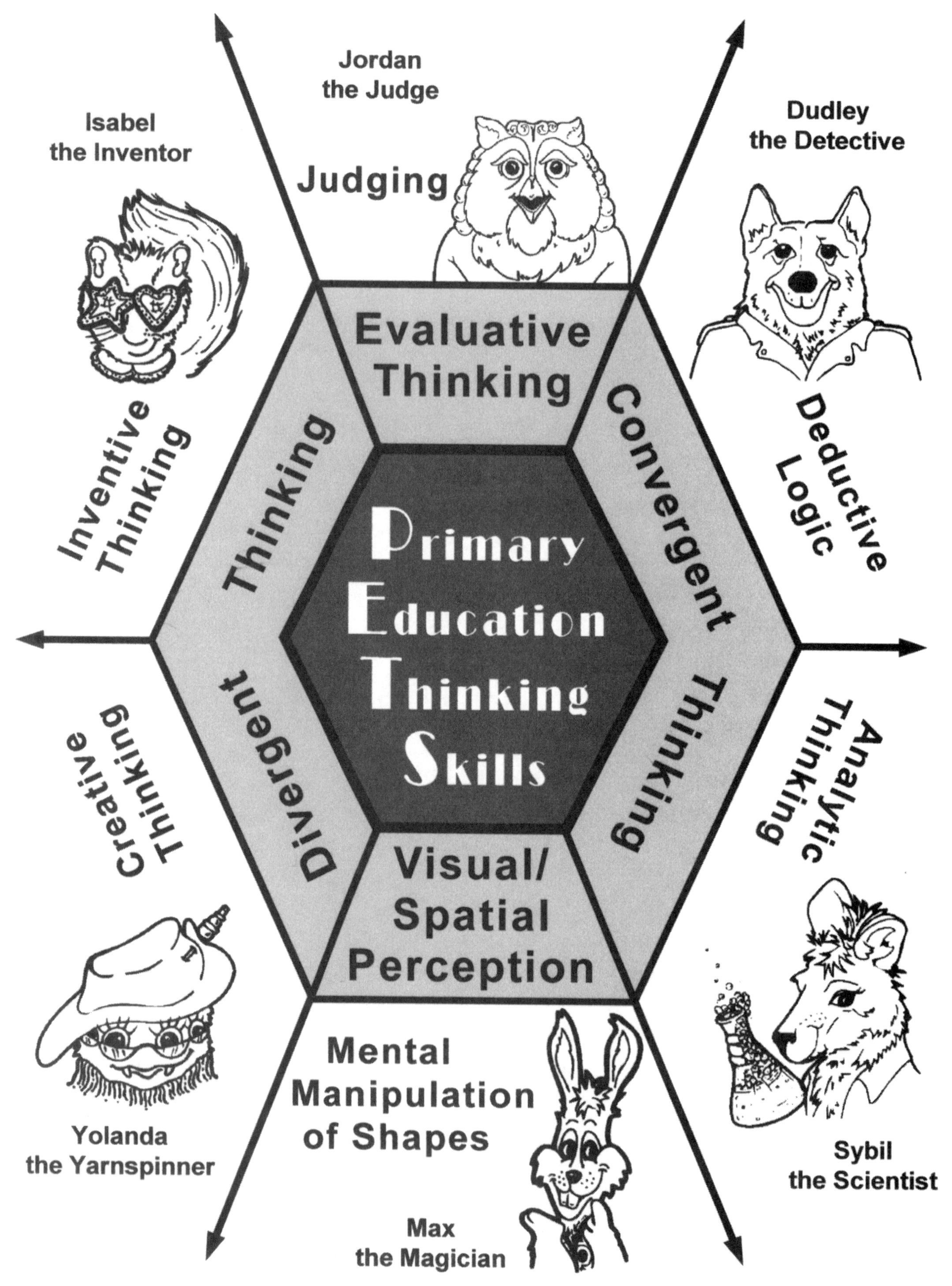
Jordan
the Judge
Isabel
the Inventor
Judging
Dudley
the Detective
Evaluative
Thinking
Inventive
Thinking
Thinking
Convergent
Deductive
Logic
Primary
Education
Thinking
Skills
Divergent
Creative
Thinking
Thinking
Analytic
Thinking
Visual/
Spatial
Perception
Mental
Manipulation
of Shapes
Yolanda
the Yarnspinner
Sybil
the Scientist
Max
the Magician

PETS™ (Primary Education Thinking Skills)

Dudley the Detective

DEFINITION

. . . is a systematized enrichment and diagnostic thinking skills program that can be easily integrated into an existing primary curriculum. PETS™ serves the dual purpose of helping in the identification of academically talented students and teaching students higher level thinking skills.

Isabel the Inventor

PROGRAM RATIONALE

Sybil the Scientist

PETS™ follows the taxonomy outlined by Benjamin Bloom, presenting lessons in analysis, synthesis, and evaluation. These higher order skills are less emphasized in most primary curricula, yet students of all ability levels have shown interest in and understanding of these different types of thinking.

Yolanda the Yarnspinner

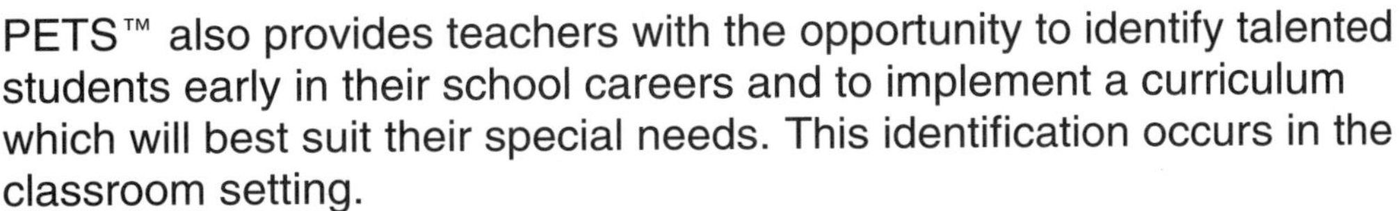

PETS™ also provides teachers with the opportunity to identify talented students early in their school careers and to implement a curriculum which will best suit their special needs. This identification occurs in the classroom setting.

Max the Magician

The format of the PETS™ delivery system follows a modification of the Triad Model posed by Dr. Joseph Renzulli. The entire class is given the opportunity to experience the challenge of the new thinking skill. Based on teacher observation and student interest, a small group of students is then given further opportunity to explore the thinking skill in a variety of in-depth activities. During the small group activities, the teacher is able to evaluate student potential further and to plan student programming accordingly.

Jordan the Judge

PETS™ IN THE 21ST CENTURY

As educators in the 21st century, we are charged with educating students to be successful in a complex, interconnected world. This responsibility requires schools to prepare students for technological, cultural, economic, informational, and demographic changes.

PETS™ supports these thinking skills as outlined in the chart below. PETS™ also aligns with the Common Core Learning Standards, as demonstrated in the chart on the following page.

PETS™ and the 21st Century Thinking Skills	Dudley	Isabel	Sybil	Yolanda	Max	Jordan
Inquire and think critically.	X	X	X	X	X	X
Apply knowledge to new situations, draw conclusions, and make informed decisions.	X	X	X	X	X	X
Share knowledge and solve problems ethically and productively as members of a multicultural world.	X	X	X	X	X	X
Demonstrate creativity, innovation, and flexibility when solving problems.	X	X	X	X	X	X
Pursue personal and aesthetic growth.	X	X	X	X	X	X

PETS™ and the Common Core Standards

Learning Areas	Standard	Common Core Initiative Site Location	Thinking Strand
www.corestandards.org			
English Language Arts Standards	Read closely to determine what the text says explicitly and to make logical inferences from it; cite specific textual evidence when writing or speaking to support conclusions drawn from the text.	College and Career Readiness Anchor Standards for Reading »Key Ideas and Details #1	Convergent/Deductive
	Delineate and evaluate the argument and specific claims in a text, including the validity of the reasoning as well as the relevance and sufficiency of the evidence.	College and Career Readiness Anchor Standards for Reading »Integration of Knowledge and Ideas #8	Evaluative
	Prepare for and participate effectively in a range of conversations and collaborations with diverse partners, building on others' ideas and expressing their own clearly and persuasively.	College and Career Readiness Anchor Standards for Speaking and Listening »Comprehension and Collaboration #1	Divergent
	Demonstrate understanding of word relationships and nuances in word meanings.	College and Career Readiness Anchor Standards for Speaking and Listening »Vocabulary Acquisition and Use #5	Divergent
Mathematics Standards	Make sense of problems and persevere in solving them.	Introduction » Standards for Mathematical Practice	Convergent/Deductive
	Reason abstractly and quantitatively.	Introduction » Standards for Mathematical Practice	Convergent/Deductive Visual/Spatial
	Construct viable arguments and critique the reasoning of others.	Introduction » Standards for Mathematical Practice	Convergent/Deductive Evaluative
	Look for and express regularity in repeated reasoning.	Introduction » Standards for Mathematical Practice	Convergent/Deductive Evaluative
	Look for and express regularity in repeated reasoning.	Grade 1 » Introduction » Standards for Mathematical Practice	Convergent/Deductive Visual/Spatial
	Reason with shapes and their attributes.	Grade 1 » Introduction » Geometry	Visual/Spatial

PROGRAM OVERVIEW

PETS™ has a two-tier delivery system which is easily facilitated by the classroom teacher or a visiting specialist. The first tier focuses on whole class enrichment activities for the entire grade level population. The second tier activities are used in small group settings to challenge the more capable students.

At the beginning of each of the six units, a character from PETS™ introduces a high level thinking skill used in his or her job to solve problems.

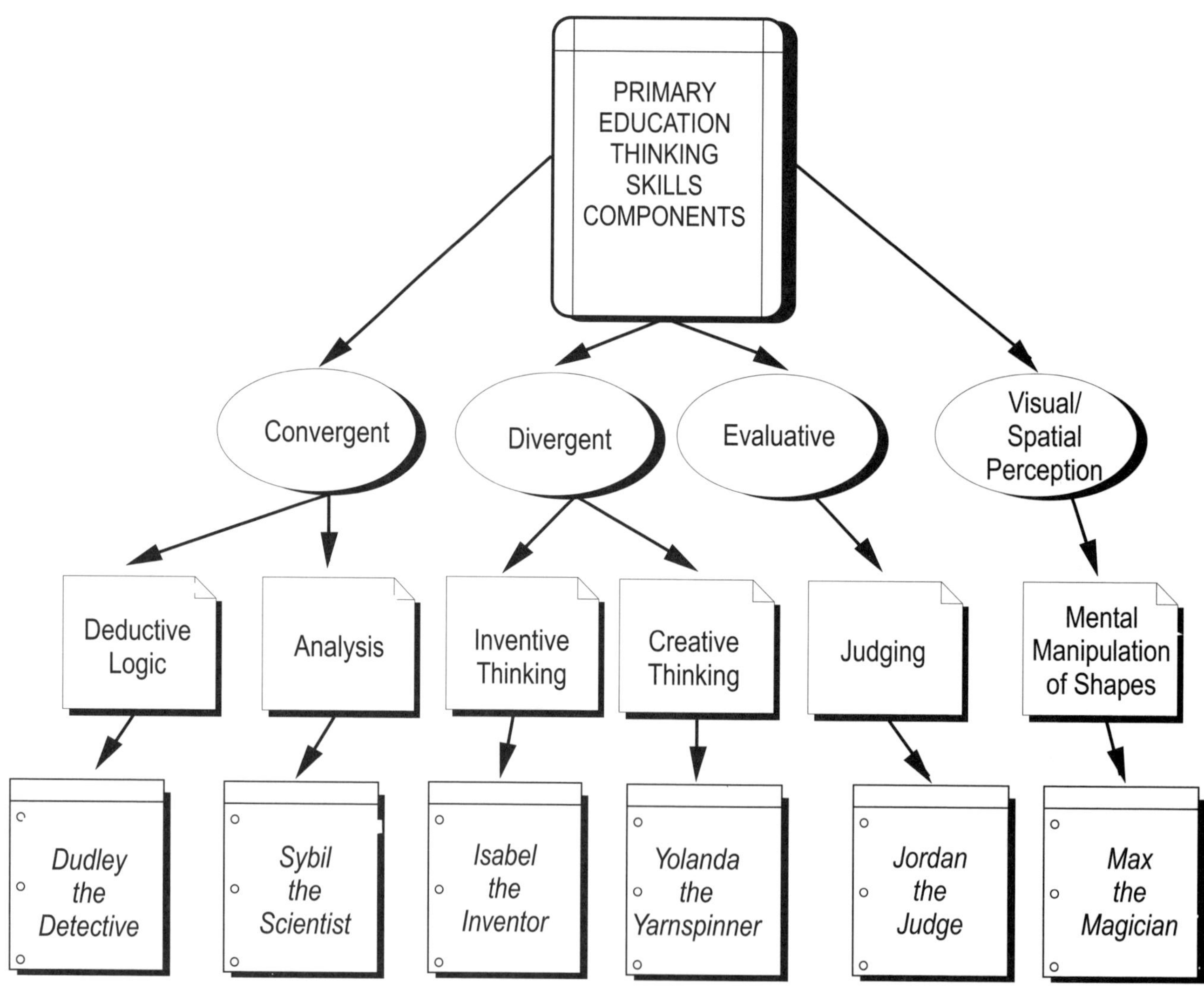

Each character serves as a guide through a story to introduce the type of thinking and a series of whole class activities to reinforce the type of thinking. Imaginative memory triggers are included with each introductory lesson.

Dudley the Detective . . . . a detective badge

Isabel the Inventor . . . . Brainfocals™

Sybil the Scientist. . . . . magnifying glass

Yolanda the Yarnspinner . . . . bookmark

Max the Magician. . . . . pencil holder

Jordan the Judge . . . . gavel

Additional activities are provided for small group sessions. These activities stimulate students with high interest, challenging exercises, many of which are hands-on. Detailed lesson plans are provided for all whole class and small group lessons. An *Ask Me What I Did Today* prompt is included with each unit to be sent home with students who participated in the small group.

Parallel to the instructional element of PETS™ is a two-tier diagnostic tool for identifying talented students. A behavioral checklist that is used by the classroom teacher during the whole group activities provides information about students who show potential. Students who show outstanding aptitude during the whole class lessons, as recorded on the checklist, are invited to participate in the small group sessions. A more detailed checklist is used during the small group sessions to better identify student levels of talent and abilities.

The PETS™ program is comprised of:

— twelve lessons for the whole class
— twelve activities for the small groups
— detailed lesson plans
— diagnostic checklists
— six *Ask Me What I Did Today* prompts

IDENTIFYING TALENTED LEARNERS

The primary classroom teacher has a very diverse population in both maturity and intellect. Some students will immediately appear talented in certain areas and other students need to be given opportunities to show their abilities. Before attempting to use the checklists, teachers need to understand the different characteristics and behaviors which indicate that a student might be talented in a particular area.

CONVERGENT THINKING

The ability to see intuitively the correct answer is one characteristic of students who excel at deductive convergent thinking. They tend to see the interrelationships between clues and defer judgment until all clues have been collected. Many times they will display outside knowledge about a topic that will help them discover the correct solution.

DIVERGENT THINKING

Those students who excel at divergent thinking are able to list many responses to questions or brainstorm many ideas. Not only are they fluent in

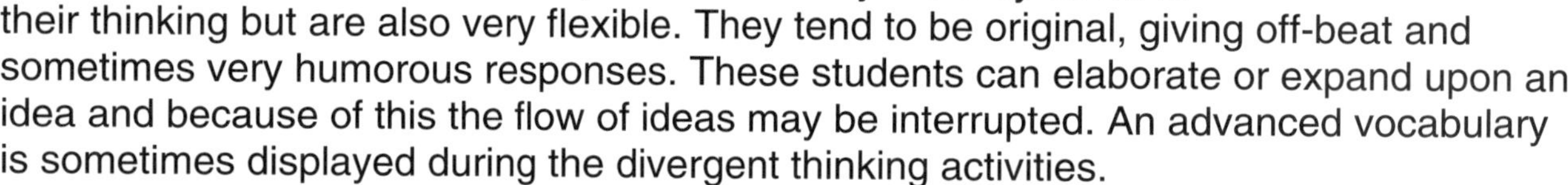

their thinking but are also very flexible. They tend to be original, giving off-beat and sometimes very humorous responses. These students can elaborate or expand upon an idea and because of this the flow of ideas may be interrupted. An advanced vocabulary is sometimes displayed during the divergent thinking activities.

VISUAL/SPATIAL PERCEPTION

These students demonstrate a good memory for detail. They may not be as verbal as their classmates and therefore may not have as much opportunity to demonstrate their talents during traditional classroom activities. These students often enjoy activities involving hands-on building of three-dimensional objects from two-dimensional drawings. During class work, these students often respond best to visual images such as graphic organizers and instructional computer programs.

EVALUATIVE THINKING

The students who are able to evaluate and offer a solution that is based on valid considerations have an opportunity to shine during these specially designed lessons. The checklists support behaviors such as seeing more than one viewpoint, understanding considerations, and supporting decisions and opinions.

IDENTIFYING TALENTED LEARNERS DURING WHOLE CLASS LESSONS

The PETS™ program can help both classroom and specialty teachers identify talented students in whole class situations and small group situations. The whole class lessons are the first tier in identifying students. The ideal situation is to have two teachers in the classroom, one teacher presenting the thinking skill lesson and one teacher observing students' behaviors. If two teachers are not available, the program will work with a parent volunteer or a teacher's aide. If this is the case, the teacher can help the aide by using key phrases to indicate that a student's name should be added to the checklist. For example a teacher may say, *"Wow, Julie, that's a great way to use an earlier clue to see the new clue."*

Seven behavior characteristics are included for each thinking skill. The sets of behaviors vary from thinking skill to thinking skill. Checklists are provided in each unit as an easy reference for teachers. As a student is observed showing one of the behaviors, the teacher records the student's name in the appropriate box. If the student shows additional behaviors in that category, the teacher can add check marks after the name. To differentiate between sessions, record each lesson's responses in a different color.

It is important for the teacher observing students to look beyond just the most vocal students who are the first to answer. All students need to be observed and questioned to give all students an opportunity to show their potential. There is a category on the behavioral checklist to indicate students who show outstanding performance on seat work or class work. The behavioral checklists also include opportunities to list students who were not present during the thinking skill lesson or have shown the characteristics in other classroom situations.

It is essential for the teacher to remember that the number of talented learners in any one classroom may be quite small. The PETS™ program has been designed to identify this small population; do not expect the entire class to achieve mastery of the lessons. All students will benefit from exposure to these higher-level thinking skills, but the actual number of students demonstrating mastery level may be quite small. That's OK.

Consider everything a child does to be diagnostic. Some children will respond enthusiastically to the intellectual challenges provided by the PETS™ whole class lessons while other children will not respond favorably. In each case, the reaction tells the teacher something about the learner.

At the end of one or two whole class thinking skill lessons, the students who are talented in that type of thinking will stand out as the teacher examines the behavioral checklist for that thinking skill. The students frequently listed on the checklist and listed in a variety of areas are the students who are invited to the small group lessons. When in doubt about a student's level of performance, include the child in the small group sessions and see how well he does – this is a time to be more inclusive than exclusive. Small group participants will often vary from thinking skill to thinking skill.

IDENTIFYING TALENTED LEARNERS DURING SMALL GROUP LESSONS

The second tier of the identification process is the small group lessons. The small group may consist of students from a variety of classrooms or a group from the same classroom.

The small group lessons are designed to provide further enrichment and opportunities for teachers to observe additional behaviors that identify talented students. Lesson plans are provided for the small group lessons. The lesson plans reflect the faster pace delivery and in-depth content appropriate for gifted students. The small group lessons are not as structured as the whole class lessons and provide students with more opportunities for interaction and cooperative problem solving. These lessons are intended to be diagnostic as opposed to instructional.

Consider everything a child does to be diagnostic. Some children will respond enthusiastically to the intellectual challenges provided by the PETS™ whole class lessons while other children will not respond favorably. In each case, the reaction tells the teacher something about the learner.

Use the form on the following page during small group lessons for record-keeping and note-taking about students.

PETS™ Small Group Checklist

A Cumulative Student Record

STUDENT: SCHOOL: TEACHER:

GRADE LEVEL:

YEAR:

+ exceeds expectations
✓ meets expectations
- below expectations

	CONVERGENT				DIVERGENT				VISUAL/ SPATIAL		EVALUA-TIVE	
	Deductive		Analytical		Inventive		Creative					
DATE												
ACTIVITY												
CHARACTERISTICS												
Comprehends concepts												
Reasons independently												
Solves puzzles/problems successfully												
Sees inter-relationships/uses clues & criteria												
Uses alternative methods to solve problems												
Enjoys puzzles/problems with a twist												
Defers judgments												
Supports evaluations effectively												
Is fluent with ideas												
Shows flexibility												
Exhibits originality												
Elaborates with many details												
Exhibits curiosity												
Displays an advanced sense of humor												
Uses an extensive vocabulary												
Demonstrates task commitment												
Demonstrates leadership												
Retains information												

COMMENTS:

INCORPORATING PETS™ INTO FORMAL SCREENING AND IDENTIFICATION OF GIFTED & TALENTED STUDENTS

A PETS™ rubric has been included for school districts that intend to incorporate PETS™ into their formal screening and identification process. Used along with traditional standardized test scores, data from PETS™ program participation generates a more inclusive picture of the talented learners in a school. Performance by individual students in small group sessions can be quantified using the scoring procedure outlined below:

1. Initially screen the student population for students who participated in at least 75% of the small group opportunities over the course of the whole program as offered by the school district.
2. Levels reflect either the grade levels at which the program was offered or the level of the PETS™ materials being used (the red book being level 1, the green book being level 2, and the blue book being level 3).
3. Scoring samples:
   A. In a 3-year program, a student who participated in the Divergent small group sessions each year (3 points), demonstrating strong effective use of divergent thinking strategies and an attitude consistent with that of a gifted learner each year (18 points), would receive a score of 21 points for Divergent thinking.
   B. In a 3-year program, a student who only participated in the Convergent small group sessions at Levels 1 and 3 (2 points), demonstrating a strong effective use of this strategy only at Level 1 (5 points) and an attitude each year consistent with that of a bright child (4 points), would receive a score of 11 points for Convergent thinking.
4. Scores for each type of thinking are finally totaled together to produce a quantitative score for use in an identification process that necessitates the use of numbers.

PETS™ IN THE REGULAR CLASSROOM

Once students have experienced the different problem-solving strategies used by the Crystal Pond Woods thinking specialists through the PETS™ program activities, it is important for students to see how these strategies work for them in "real" life. Using the language of these specialists in the context of core classroom curricula whenever possible makes concrete connections for students and anchors these concepts more effectively in their minds. The chart on page 16 is designed for teachers to use when mapping out daily lessons/activities:

- What are you teaching?
- What thinking skill/s will it entail?
- Which Crystal Pond Woods character specializes in those strategies?

PETS™ Rubric

Date:

Students	Divergent				Convergent				Evaluative				Visual				Total
	Level			Score	Level			Score	Level			Score	Level			Score	
	1	2	3		1	2	3		1	2	3		1	2	3		

RUBRIC	3	2	1	0
	Small groups at all levels	Small groups at two levels	Small group at one level	No small groups
	Strong effective use of this thinking strategy	Effective use of this thinking strategy	Minimal effective use of this thinking strategy	No effective use of this thinking strategy
	Usually demonstrated attitude consistent with that of a gifted learner	Sometimes demonstrated attitude consistent with that of a gifted learner	Demonstrated attitude consistent with that of a bright child	Demonstrated attitude consistent with that of a good student

PETS™ IN THE REGULAR CLASSROOM

LESSON/ACTIVITY	THINKING SKILL/S	THINKING SPECIALIST/S
		❑ Dudley/Detective ❑ Sybil/Scientist ❑ Isabel/Inventor ❑ Yolanda/Yarnspinner ❑ Max/Magician ❑ Jordan/Judge

Notes:

LESSON/ACTIVITY	THINKING SKILL/S	THINKING SPECIALIST/S
		❑ Dudley/Detective ❑ Sybil/Scientist ❑ Isabel/Inventor ❑ Yolanda/Yarnspinner ❑ Max/Magician ❑ Jordan/Judge

Notes:

LESSON/ACTIVITY	THINKING SKILL/S	THINKING SPECIALIST/S
		❑ Dudley/Detective ❑ Sybil/Scientist ❑ Isabel/Inventor ❑ Yolanda/Yarnspinner ❑ Max/Magician ❑ Jordan/Judge

Notes:

Dudley the Detective

. . . Uses

clues

. . . To find one

and only one

right answer

Convergent/Deductive Thinking

List names of students as each behavior appears. **Add checkmarks** after name if behavior is repeated. **Use a different color** of ink or pencil for each whole group lesson.	**PETS™** **Behavioral Checklist** **Detective Thinking** (deductive logic/convergent thinking)	Teacher ______________ Grade _____ Dates of whole group instruction: 1. ______ 2. ______

GRASPS CONCEPTS QUICKLY	**SEES INTERRELATIONSHIP OF CLUES;** PUTS CLUES TOGETHER; USES ONE CLUE TO DETERMINE ANOTHER
DRAWS RELATIONSHIPS BETWEEN LESSON & OUTSIDE INFORMATION TO HELP DETERMINE CONCLUSIONS	**DEFERS JUDGMENT;** CONSIDERS ALL INFORMATION BEFORE COMING TO A CONCLUSION
SEES ANSWERS INTUITIVELY WITHOUT INTERMEDIATE STEPS	**IS TENACIOUS** IN APPROACH; WORKS DILIGENTLY TO THE END
RETAINS INFORMATION FROM PREVIOUS LESSONS	**PETS™ CLASSWORK** INDICATES AN OUTSTANDING ABILITY TO USE THIS THINKING SKILL

I see these behaviors in these students regularly during class time as well:	These students did not stand out during the PETS™ lessons, but I see these behaviors during regular class time:	Notes:

DIAGNOSTIC NOTES • DETECTIVE THINKING

<table>
<tr><td>GRASPS CONCEPTS QUICKLY

♦ applies the process of elimination
♦ first to figure out correct answers</td><td>SEES INTERRELATIONSHIP OF CLUES; PUTS CLUES TOGETHER; USES ONE CLUE TO DETERMINE ANOTHER

♦ combines information from various clues to determine the correct solution</td></tr>
<tr><td>DRAWS RELATIONSHIPS BETWEEN LESSON & OUTSIDE INFORMATION TO HELP DETERMINE CONCLUSIONS

♦ uses knowledge from outside class effectively as clues</td><td>DEFERS JUDGMENT; CONSIDERS ALL INFORMATION BEFORE COMING TO A CONCLUSION

♦ waits until enough information is gathered to work out the right answer
♦ avoids guessing impulsively</td></tr>
<tr><td>SEES ANSWERS INTUITIVELY WITHOUT INTERMEDIATE STEPS

♦ arrives at correct answer without seeming to use intermediate steps
♦ not an impulsive guesser</td><td>IS TENACIOUS IN APPROACH; WORKS DILIGENTLY TO THE END

♦ works diligently to conclusion
♦ will NOT give up</td></tr>
<tr><td>RETAINS INFORMATION FROM PREVIOUS LESSONS

♦ shares knowledge accurately during review
♦ applies knowledge during activities</td><td>PETS™ CLASSWORK INDICATES AN OUTSTANDING ABILITY TO USE THIS THINKING SKILL

♦ seatwork and/or challenge papers are exceptionally well done</td></tr>
</table>

I see these behaviors in these students regularly during class time as well:	These students did not stand out during the PETS™ lessons, but I see these behaviors during regular class time:	Notes:
♦ *normally great convergent thinkers*	♦ *normally great convergent thinkers who "hid out" during the PETS™ lesson*	♦ *absentees* ♦ *new students*

- *be generous — more inclusive than exclusive*
- *names can go in more than one box per answer*
- *be sure to add ✓s after names for multiple answers*
- *be sure to use different colors for each whole group lessor*

DETECTIVE THINKING
WHOLE CLASS
LESSON 1

PURPOSE

The purpose of this lesson is to introduce the students to **deductive convergent thinking**. The students will be introduced to *Dudley the Detective* who puts his clues together to arrive at the one correct answer to the problem. The students should be made to understand that in deductive convergent thinking:

— There is one and only one right answer.
— They must find and read all the clues.
— They may not see the answer right away and need to reflect on some of the clues.
— They may need to put together many pieces of information in order to find the one right answer.
— Patience is important in not jumping to conclusions and in reflecting on clues.

TEACHER MATERIALS

For projection:

— *Dudley the Detective* picture – a colorized Dudley is available on the CD
— *Mystery Creatures*

For duplication:

— *Dudley the Detective* story to read aloud
— *Mystery Creatures* story to read aloud
— *PETS™ Behavioral Checklist – Detective Thinking*
— picture of Dudley the Detective for each student to color
— class set of *Mystery Creatures*
— class set of *Who Is Mary?*
— class set of *Which Dog Belongs To Mary?*
— class set of detective badges, perhaps run on yellow or goldenrod paper

— pins or masking tape for the badges

STUDENT MATERIALS

— crayons or colored pencils
— pencils
— scissors

LESSON PLAN

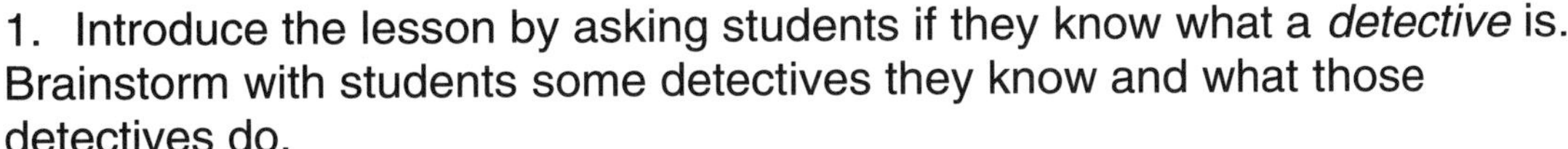

1. Introduce the lesson by asking students if they know what a *detective* is. Brainstorm with students some detectives they know and what those detectives do.

2. Tell the students that today they are going to meet Dudley the Detective who thinks in a very special way when solving problems. Project the picture of Dudley. Students may color their pictures of Dudley at this time or following the reading of the story.

3. Read the story, *Dudley the Detective.*

4. Review with students these points from the story:
   — In deductive thinking, there is only one right answer.
   — Clues must be found and then read before they can be used.
   — It is often necessary to put more than one clue together in order to find the needed information to solve the problem.
   — Patience is important when thinking about the clues. Reflecting on and delaying judgment of certain information is necessary. Avoid jumping to conclusions or relying on pre-conceived notions.

5. Help the students cut out and make detective badges, the memory trigger for this unit. Have them label the badges with their names or with a creative detective name if you prefer. The students may wear their badges while doing the deductive activities.

6. Distribute *Mystery Creatures* worksheets. While wearing their badges, have the students listen to the *Mystery Creatures* story. Following the clues outlined in the story, students should draw in the boxes on their worksheets the creatures they think are being described and label the kind of animal each one is. Remind them that these are REAL creatures and fantasy drawings should be avoided.

CHALLENGE PAGES

Who is Mary?
Which Dog Belongs to Mary?

7. Distribute the challenge pages to students. Read the clues aloud to non-reading students as needed. If students have the reading ability, the challenge pages can be assigned as independent work. If the challenge pages are going to be used for assessing student potential, it is important that students work on them independently in class. Have students stand up folders on their desks to protect their privacy. Tell them that they are "private detectives" who may only share their work with their immediate supervisor – their teacher!

ANSWER KEY

Mystery Creatures 1. turtle 2. owl 3. bear 4. fox

Who Is Mary?

Name

Who Is Mary?

Dudley is looking for Mary. Use these clues to help you find Mary. Color her.

1. Mary has long hair.
2. Mary does **not** play with dolls.

Mary is happ

4. Mary likes to ska

Which Dog Belongs To Mary?

Name

Which Dog Belongs To Mary?

Use these clues to help you find Mary's dog. Color it.

1. Its tail is long.
2. It is **not** a big dog.
3. It does **not** have spots.
4. Its ears are like its tail.

DIAGNOSTIC NOTES

During this lesson, the teacher and observer will be looking for students who display specific characteristics. These students will then be invited to the small group sessions for additional activities. Some teachers explain the structure of the PETS™ curriculum to the students before actually starting the lessons. During the explanation, the teacher might point out to students the importance of volunteering during the lessons. This is the main opportunity for the teachers to know what students are thinking and students need to share their thoughts.

Characteristic behaviors and responses are listed on the PETS™ behavioral checklists, one checklist for each of the six units. There is an overlap of characteristics among the units. The following is a short summary of what student behaviors and responses to note during the Detective Thinking unit.

GRASPS CONCEPTS QUICKLY – Look for students who quickly understand and use the process of elimination. List the students who are the first to figure out the correct answers.

SEES INTERRELATIONSHIP OF CLUES – Look for students who build one clue's information on a previous clue to deduce the answer.

DRAWS RELATIONSHIPS BETWEEN THE LESSON AND OUTSIDE INFORMATION – Look for students who exhibit knowledge from outside the classroom and use it as an additional clue in solving the puzzle. After the lesson is over, students should be noted who see the relationship between thinking like detectives and other classroom activities.

DEFERS JUDGMENT – Look for students who wait until they have figured out the correct answer. These students avoid guessing until they determine the correct answer.

SEES ANSWERS INTUITIVELY – Some students who are excellent convergent thinkers are unable to verbalize how they figured out the answer. Note students when this occurs.

IS TENACIOUS – In addition to watching for students who work diligently to the end of the activities, note students who want to work on convergent-type activities. An enthusiasm towards this type of problem often indicates an ability to solve these problems.

RETAINS INFORMATION – When reviewing ideas from earlier lessons, look for students who clearly recall the concepts and then effectively apply them to the current lesson's activities. While many children may grasp concepts "in the moment" of the instructional lesson, these students exhibit the significant ability to retain and apply new learning across time.

Who Is Mary? and ***Which Dog Belongs To Mary?***

Look for students who:

– solve the puzzles correctly.

NOTES

Dudley The Detective

One bright, sunny morning, Dudley the Detective woke up, stretched, and yawned.

"What a GREAT morning," he thought to himself. "This will be a fine day for solving a mystery."

Dudley is a detective. He *loves* to solve mysteries. He *loves* to spend his mornings **looking for** and **finding clues**, then **reading** what they tell him about the latest mystery in town.

Dudley's favorite afternoons are spent **thinking** about all the information he has gathered. He's always careful **not to jump to conclusions**. He prefers to ponder a mystery until after dinner.

Once Dudley has eaten dinner, the phone will begin to ring, for all the folks in town know that Dudley will have figured out the **one** correct answer while doing his dishes. He'll exclaim,

"I'VE GOT IT!!"

As Dudley stretched and yawned on this particular morning, he realized that he did not have a mystery to solve today! "How disappointing," he thought to himself, but he put on his detective uniform anyway.

First, Dudley slipped on his trench coat, since many detectives wear trench coats. Then he put his magnifying glass in his coat pocket. Detectives need magnifying glasses to search *carefully* for clues.

The only thing Dudley needed now to be ready for a good mystery was his detective badge. Dudley had received this very special gold badge for graduating from his detective school with honors!

As he searched his room, however, Dudley could not find his badge anywhere! He looked high. He looked low. He looked to the left. He looked to the right. He looked *everywhere*, but his detective badge was *not* to be found.

This was definitely a very distressing situation, but Dudley knew that he was the *best* detective in the Woods, so if *any*one could find his badge, certainly *he* was the one.

The first thing Dudley needed to do was to **find some clues**. He noticed that his window was open. He also saw muddy paw prints in his room that appeared to be those of a raccoon. Dudley knew that Rascal Raccoon often got into trouble, but Dudley did not want to jump to the wrong conclusion, so he continued looking for clues.

Outside, Dudley found more paw prints going up and over his fence towards Rascal Raccoon's house next door. As Dudley continued his search for clues, he had to shade his eyes from the bright sunlight that was reflecting off an old apple tree in his backyard. Later, out of the corner of his eye, he noticed his friend, Rosalyn Robin, returning to her nest in that old tree. However, after looking all over the yard and even back inside his house, Dudley still had not found his badge.

After lunch, Dudley sat down to think about the case. It seemed like Rascal Raccoon was the likely culprit, but Dudley knew he **should not jump to a quick conclusion**, so he continued to ponder the mystery during dinner. Carefully he **thought** about each of the clues he had found.

(At this time, ask the students what clues Dudley has found to help him solve this mystery before returning to the story to see if Dudley's figured things out yet ....)

Dudley was washing his dishes after dinner when he suddenly burst out, "I've GOT it!"

(At this time, ask the students, "Do you think you've got it?)

Dudley rushed outside and got out his ladder from the tool shed. He carried it over to the apple tree, and then he climbed up to the spot from which the sunlight had been reflecting so brightly into his eyes earlier that day!

Sure enough, there in Rosalyn Robin's nest was Dudley's missing detective badge. Rosalyn admitted to seeing the beautiful shiny object in Dudley's house and to flying in that open window to take the special badge.

Rascal Raccoon had been in Dudley's house, too, but not to take the detective badge. That was a mystery that Dudley would have to save for another day!

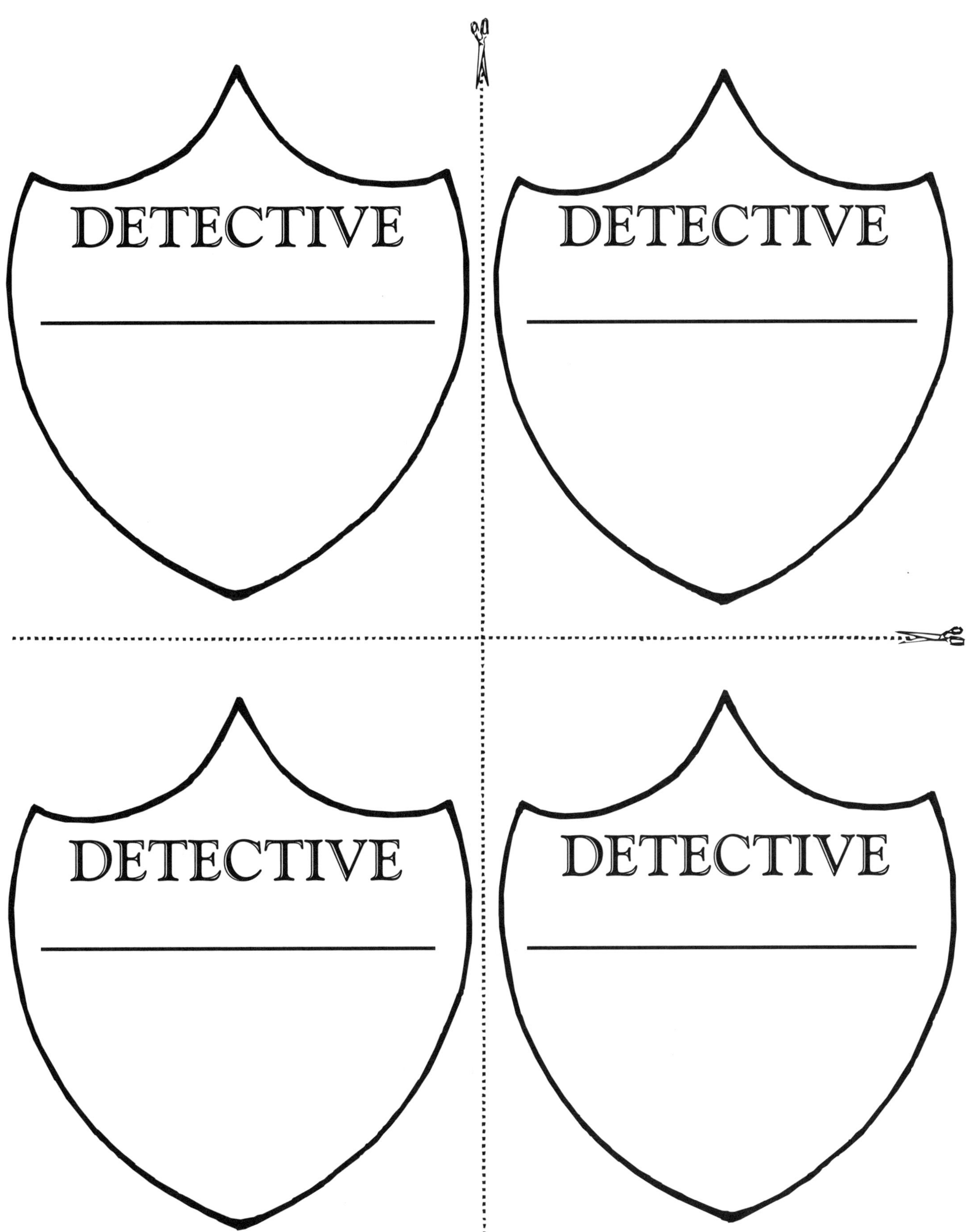
DETECTIVE
DETECTIVE
DETECTIVE
DETECTIVE

MYSTERY CREATURES

Dudley, Rosalyn Robin, and their friends in Crystal Pond Woods have another mystery for you to solve. Here are descriptions of four real animals. Three are friends and live in the woods. The fourth one is a mysterious stranger. Listen to the clues and help Dudley figure out who is who by drawing what you think these creatures look like. Write down the kind of animal you drew.

1. My favorite afternoons are spent sunning on a log by the pond. When Rascal Raccoon comes by, I ignore him by pulling my head, tail, and four feet into "my house."

2. Some say I am very wise. Maybe that's because when I'm not flying I can turn my head almost all the way around. I don't miss much. I'm also forever asking one question.

3. My love for honey sometimes gets me into a whole lot of trouble. When I stick my paw into the beehive, I usually get stung on my black nose. My brown fur helps to protect me everywhere else.

4. I'm afraid Rosalyn Robin spotted me last night sneaking through the woods. I'm sure she noticed my pointy ears and long red bushy tail. I know she does not feel safe while I'm around. She needn't worry — even though my legs are short, I can travel very quickly, and I'll be gone by dawn.

Name ______________________________________

Mystery Creatures

Mystery Creature #1	Mystery Creature #2
Kind of animal:	Kind of animal:

Mystery Creature #3	Mystery Creature #4
Kind of animal:	Kind of animal:

Name ______________________________

Who Is Mary?

Dudley is looking for Mary. Use these clues to help you find Mary. Color her.

1. Mary has long hair.
2. Mary does ***not*** play with dolls.
3. Mary is happy.
4. Mary likes to skate.

Name ______________________

Which Dog Belongs To Mary?

Use these clues to help you find Mary's dog. Color it.

1. Its tail is long.
2. It is ***not*** a big dog.
3. It does ***not*** have spots.
4. Its ears are like its tail.

DETECTIVE THINKING
WHOLE CLASS
LESSON 2

PURPOSE

The purpose of this lesson is to review and reinforce the concepts of **deductive convergent thinking.** Students will use clues to deduce the correct answers to a series of questions. Remind students that:

- There is one and only one right answer.
- They must find and read all the clues.
- They may need to put together many pieces of information in order to find the one right answer.
- They may need to reflect on some of the clues since they may not see the answer right away.
- They need to refrain from jumping to conclusions.

TEACHER MATERIALS

For projection:

- *A Party in the Woods*
- *Lost Toys*
- *Who Gets Which Gift?*

For duplication:

- *PETS™ Behavioral Checklist – Detective Thinking*
- class set of *Ladybug Leap*
- class set of *Color the Flowers*

STUDENT MATERIALS

- crayons or colored pencils
- pencils

LESSON PLAN

1. Review with students the concepts introduced by Dudley the Detective in Lesson 1. Discuss with students the characteristics of a *detective.*

2. Tell students that they are going to be detectives today. Project a copy of *A Party in the Woods.* Give students an opportunity to study the scene before discussing the picture. This scene has pictures of most of the main characters in the PETS™ program. During this lesson, use the name of each character. (See the third discussion question below.)

3. The following are questions the teacher should ask students as they study *A Party in the Woods*. The questions do not have to be asked in order. The discussion can evolve as students make observations and inferences based on the clues. The answers are provided in italics. As students give you answers, ask them what they see to support their conclusions.

DISCUSSION QUESTIONS

- What celebration is going on here? *(A birthday party.)*
- How can you tell? *(There is a cake with candles – this is the defining clue that must be recognized as birthdays are the only celebrations that have cakes with candles. Presents, entertainment, and decorations are clues that indicate a party, but not necessarily a birthday party.)*
- Someone at the party is named Bill. Who do you think it is? Why? *(He is the boy with the fishing pole. His name is on his shirt, but only the "LL" is visible. This is a good time to identify everyone else at the party:*
  - o *Dudley the Detective, the dog*
  - o *Isabel the Inventor, the squirrel*
  - o *Sybil the Scientist, the kangaroo*
  - o *Yolanda the Yarns pinner, the spider*
  - o *Max the Magician, the rabbit*
  - o *Jordan the Judge, the owl*
  - o *Betty, Bill's friend*
  - o *Baby Bear*
  - o *Felix Fish*
- Whose birthday is it? How can you tell? *(The owl's, Jordan the Judge, because he is by the cake that has many, many candles on it – the defining clues. Students usually focus on Baby Bear who is also by the cake, but that is the only evidence that supports the bear. There is a gift tag with the name "Owl" on it, but it is not clear if the gift is to Owl or from Owl.)*
- What season is it? *(It is autumn because there are only a few leaves left on the trees, there are leaves on the ground, and it is still warm enough not to need a coat.)*
- What do you think Bill is going to do at the party? Why? *(He has a fishing pole, and there is a pond with fish in it so he is probably going fishing.)*
- Sybil the Scientist has just arrived at the party. What do you think her present might be? Why? *(The present might be soft or something curved. It is also light enough to carry. Accept any reasonable answers which fit.)*
- What other things are going on at the party? *(It appears that Max the Magician is putting on a magic show. Some of the other things brought up by students can be accepted if they are supported by clues or evidence in the picture.)*

4. After completing the discussion, project *Lost Toys* and *Who Gets Which Gift?* Work through these "mysteries" as a class.

CHALLENGE PAGES

Ladybug Leap
Color the Flowers

5. Distribute the challenge pages to students. Read the clues aloud to non-reading students as needed. If students have the reading ability, the challenge pages can be assigned as independent work. If the challenge pages are going to be used for assessing student potential, it is important that students work independently and complete the pages at school. Have students stand up folders on their desks to protect their privacy. Tell them that they are "private detectives" who may only share their work with their immediate supervisor – their teacher!

ANSWER KEY

Lost Toys	(1) Brad (2) Bill (3) Betty (4) Brenda (5) Beth
Who Gets Which Gift?	Isabel, Max, Yolanda, Dudley, Jordan Jordan gets the biggest gift.
Ladybug Leap	(1) 9 (2) 15 (3) 6 (4) 2 (5) 12
Color the Flowers	(l-r) purple, yellow, orange, blue, red

DIAGNOSTIC NOTES

Characteristic behaviors and responses are listed on the PETS™ behavioral checklists, one checklist for each of the six units. There is an overlap of characteristics among the units. The following is a short summary of what student behaviors and responses to note during the Detective Thinking unit.

GRASPS CONCEPTS QUICKLY – Look for students who quickly understand and use the process of elimination. List the students who are the first to figure out the correct answers.

SEES INTERRELATIONSHIP OF CLUES – Look for students who build one clue's information on a previous clue to deduce the answer.

DRAWS RELATIONSHIPS BETWEEN THE LESSON AND OUTSIDE INFORMATION – Look for students who exhibit knowledge from outside the classroom and use it as an additional clue in solving the puzzle. After the lesson is over, students should be noted who see the relationship between thinking like detectives and other classroom activities.

DEFERS JUDGMENT – Look for students who wait until they have figured out the correct answer. These students avoid guessing until they determine the correct answer.

SEES ANSWERS INTUITIVELY – Some students who are excellent convergent thinkers are unable to verbalize how they figured out the answer. Note students when this occurs.

IS TENACIOUS – In addition to watching for students who work diligently to the end of the activities, note students who want to work on convergent-type activities. An enthusiasm towards this type of problem often indicates an ability to solve these problems.

RETAINS INFORMATION – When reviewing ideas from earlier lessons, look for students who clearly recall the concepts and then effectively apply them to the current lesson's activities. While many children may grasp concepts "in the moment" of the instructional lesson, these students exhibit the significant ability to retain and apply new learning across time.

Ladybug Leap and ***Color the Flowers***
Look for students who:
- solve the puzzles correctly.

NOTES

A Party In The Woods
OWL
CRYSTAL POND

Lost Toys

Dudley found some lost toys in Crystal Pond Woods. He wants to return them to the rightful owners. Read all the clues and write the owner's name by each toy.

1. Betty does not play with balls.
2. Bill likes to build with blocks.
3. Beth's toy is **not** round.
4. Brenda has a toy.
5. Brad loves to read.

Who Gets Which Gift?

Write the proper names on the gift tags.

1. Max's gift is **not** on top.
2. Yolanda gets the gift **right below** Max's.
3. Dudley's gift is long and thin.
4. Jordan gets a gift.
5. Isabel's gift has **two** bows.

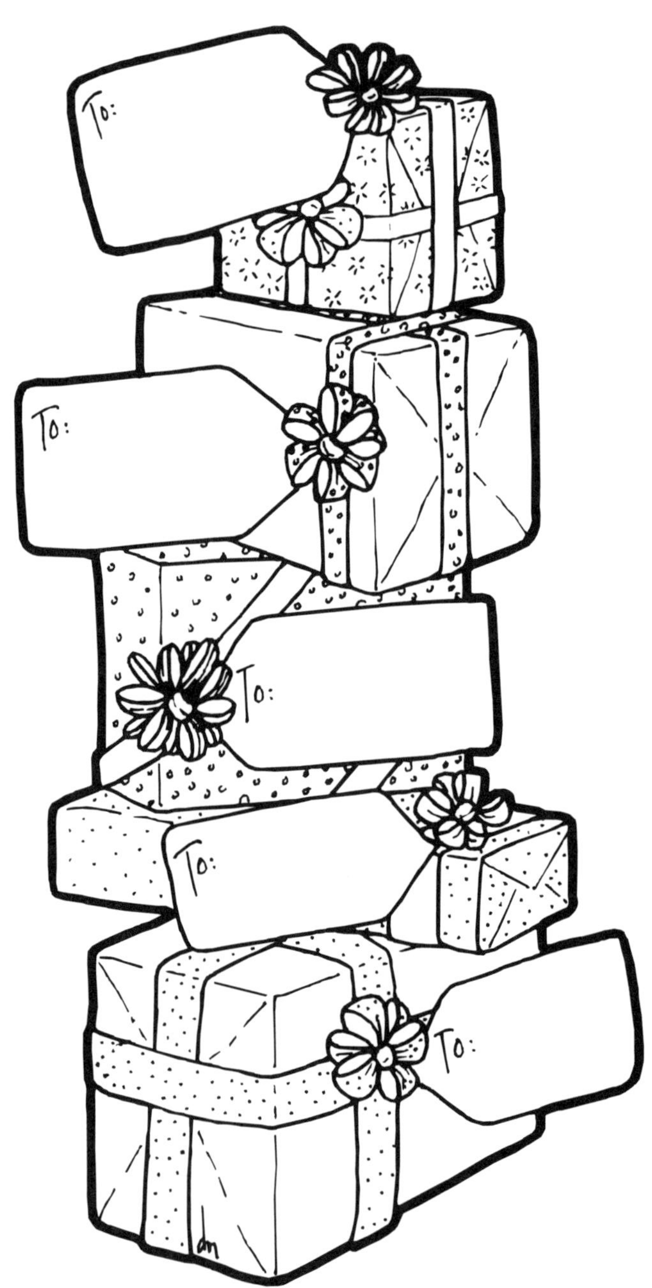

Who gets the biggest gift?

____

Name ______________________________

Ladybug Leap

Five ladybugs are racing to the tip of the leaf. Put the correct number of spots on the back of each ladybug. Write the number of spots on the line by each ladybug.

1. The 15-spotted ladybug came in second.
2. The 6-spotted ladybug did not finish last.
3. The 12-spotted one finished right behind the one with 2 spots.
4. The 9-spotted ladybug is the fastest.
5. The last 3 ladybugs have even numbers of spots.

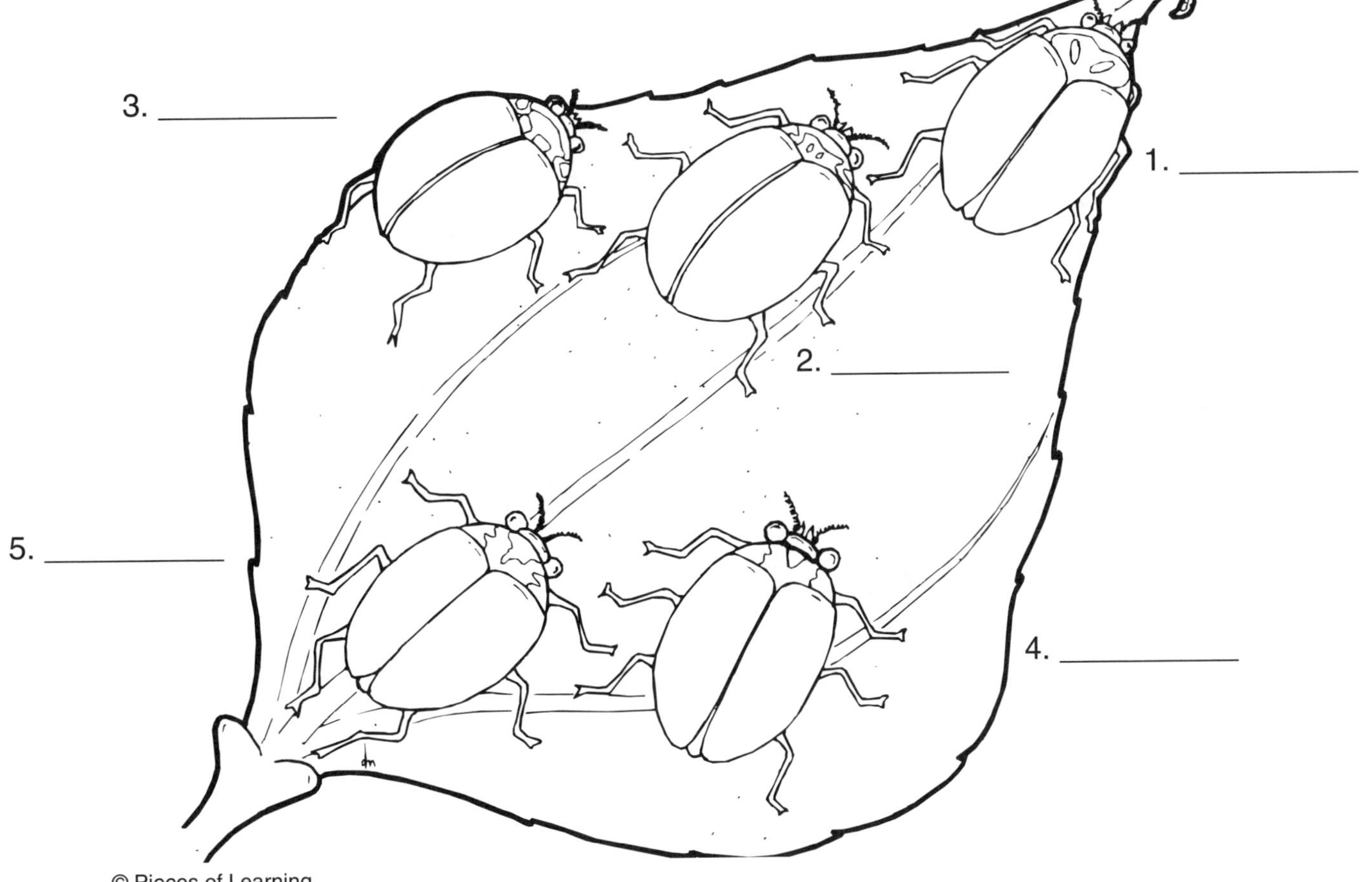

Name ______________________________

Color The Flowers

Use these clues to help color the flowers in Crystal Pond Woods.

1. The biggest flower is yellow.
2. The blue flower is not on the end.
3. The orange flower is between the yellow one and the blue one.
4. One flower is purple.
5. The smallest flower is red.

DETECTIVE THINKING SMALL GROUP LESSON 1

PURPOSE

The purpose of this lesson is to give students an opportunity to practice **deductive thinking.** Students will be using the attribute blocks. During the lesson, the teacher will be observing and assessing students as one means of identifying potentially talented learners.

TEACHER MATERIALS

For duplication:

— *PETS™ Small Group Checklist* for each student
— *Can you find your way through Crystal Pond Woods?* for each student

— a set of attribute blocks for each student. Directions are provided for making sets. A master copy of the shapes is also provided. Commercial sets are available and some die-cut machines have attribute block dies.

LESSON PLAN

1. Spread sets of attribute blocks on a table, one set in front of each student. Secretly take one block from each set and hide it. Take a different block from each student's set so each one has to figure out the solution.

2. Introduce the word *ATTRIBUTE*. Discuss that attributes are characteristics of something. Ask students what are some characteristics or attributes about themselves. Students' characteristics may include hair color, eye color, height, gender, etc., but should not include what they are wearing. Discuss why not. Then ask students to determine the characteristics of the attribute blocks.

Attributes of the blocks which should be suggested by the students are:

size -	big and little
thickness-	thin and thick
color -	blue, red, or yellow
shape -	triangle, square, hexagon, circle, rectangle

Have students hold up each shape, compare thin with thick, and compare large with small blocks of the same shape.

3. Tell students that each block has a special name of its own, which comes from naming each of its four attributes. Have students hold up their BIG, THICK, BLUE HEXAGON. (Make sure to ask for examples which are not in the student set.)

4. Next, tell students that they are going to practice their detective thinking by solving a mystery. Tell them that one block is missing from each set and will only be returned to its set when it is named correctly using each of the four attributes.

Note the processes students use in order to solve this problem. Some students may visualize and determine in their heads the missing block. Other students may manually group the blocks to determine the missing one.

If students name an incorrect block, one which is still in their sets, simply point to the incorrect choice on the table and say, *"There is your (choice of block). If you have it on the table, I cannot have it. Try to gather more clues."*

Students may at first try to guess randomly, but they will see in time that they need to group their blocks in order to determine the missing one. Do not encourage this. Allow them to arrive at this conclusion on their own.

5. As students accurately name and receive their blocks, set each student to the next task: to build one-difference trains. In this activity, students will use the attributes as clues to determine deductively which blocks correctly follow each other when building different attribute trains.

Select one block from a student's set and place it on the table in front of her. Name that block with the student. *("This is your BIG, THIN, RED SQUARE.")* Tell the student that now she is going to use her detective thinking to solve the problem of creating a train of seven or more blocks behind this block, and she must use the blocks' attributes as clues in order to do it correctly since each new block must have one, and <u>only</u> one, attribute change from the previous block.

For example, if the student's train begins with the BIG, THIN, RED SQUARE, she could place the <u>LITTLE</u>, THIN, RED SQUARE next or the BIG, <u>THICK</u>, RED SQUARE or any BIG, THIN, RED <u>SHAPE</u>. The third step of the train should be one attribute different from the second, and so on.

When the student thinks she has completed the train correctly, you will check the train by asking:

"What did you change from here to here?" (pointing to the first and second blocks). *"And from here to here?"* (pointing to the second and third blocks) and so on down the train to the end.

If the student has placed an incorrect block, help her see that she has changed too many attributes and the train should be corrected from that point. Don't have the student start over. Simply change the blocks as necessary.

6. When the student successfully completes a one-difference train, ask her to try a two-difference train, which is the same as a one-difference train except there are two new attributes at each step.

7. When a two-difference train has been successfully accomplished, have the students try circular one-difference trains. At each step, one attribute is changed, but the train makes a circle instead of a straight line so that the last block must also be one attribute different from the original block in the train. Two-difference circular trains may also be attempted.

8. Should anyone finish all the trains described above, have the student attempt to make a figure-eight train of one or two attribute differences. Place a block on the table, and tell the student that this is the center of a figure eight. The student should add four blocks above this one and four blocks below this one, so that when the "eight" shape is drawn, the center block is crossed going from the top of the eight to the bottom and again going back up from the bottom to the top. Each time the center block is crossed, it must have the correct number of attribute differences. This is a challenging activity for primary students.

9. Give each student a copy of *Can you find your way through Crystal Pond Woods?* Explain that an attribute block goes in each circle. The number of lines between the circles indicates the number of attribute changes between the circles.

DIAGNOSTIC NOTES

Some students may not be able to complete all of the activities. Look for students who:

- — grasp the concepts quickly.
- — move through all the activities.
- — create their own trains or designs with the attribute blocks.

NOTES

Attribute Blocks

Student sets of attribute blocks can be made by cutting out the shapes found on the next page. These sets will have three (3) attributes: shape, size, and color.

To add the color attribute, color one of each different shape red, one blue, and one yellow. These sets will each contain thirty (30) blocks, one each of the following:

large blue rectangle	large yellow rectangle	small red rectangle
large blue square	large yellow square	small red square
large blue circle	large yellow circle	small red circle
large blue triangle	large yellow triangle	small red triangle
large blue hexagon	large yellow hexagon	small red hexagon

large red rectangle	small blue rectangle	small yellow rectangle
large red square	small blue square	small yellow square
large red circle	small blue circle	small yellow circle
large red triangle	small blue triangle	small yellow triangle
large red hexagon	small blue hexagon	small yellow hexagon

For greater durability: Laminate pages after the shapes have been colored before they are cut out; and/or glue pages onto poster board before the shapes are cut out.

Commercial sets of attribute blocks have four (4) attributes: shape, size, color, and thickness. These sets contain sixty (60) blocks.

To add the thickness attribute to the above student sets, glue two sheets of poster board together plus the page of shapes for the thick blocks, and use one thickness of poster board and the shapes page for the thin blocks.

It is recommended that poster board block pieces be laminated to help thick pieces stay together and to keep pieces clean and in good shape.

An Attribute Blocks Set To Make

Can you find your way through Crystal Pond Woods?

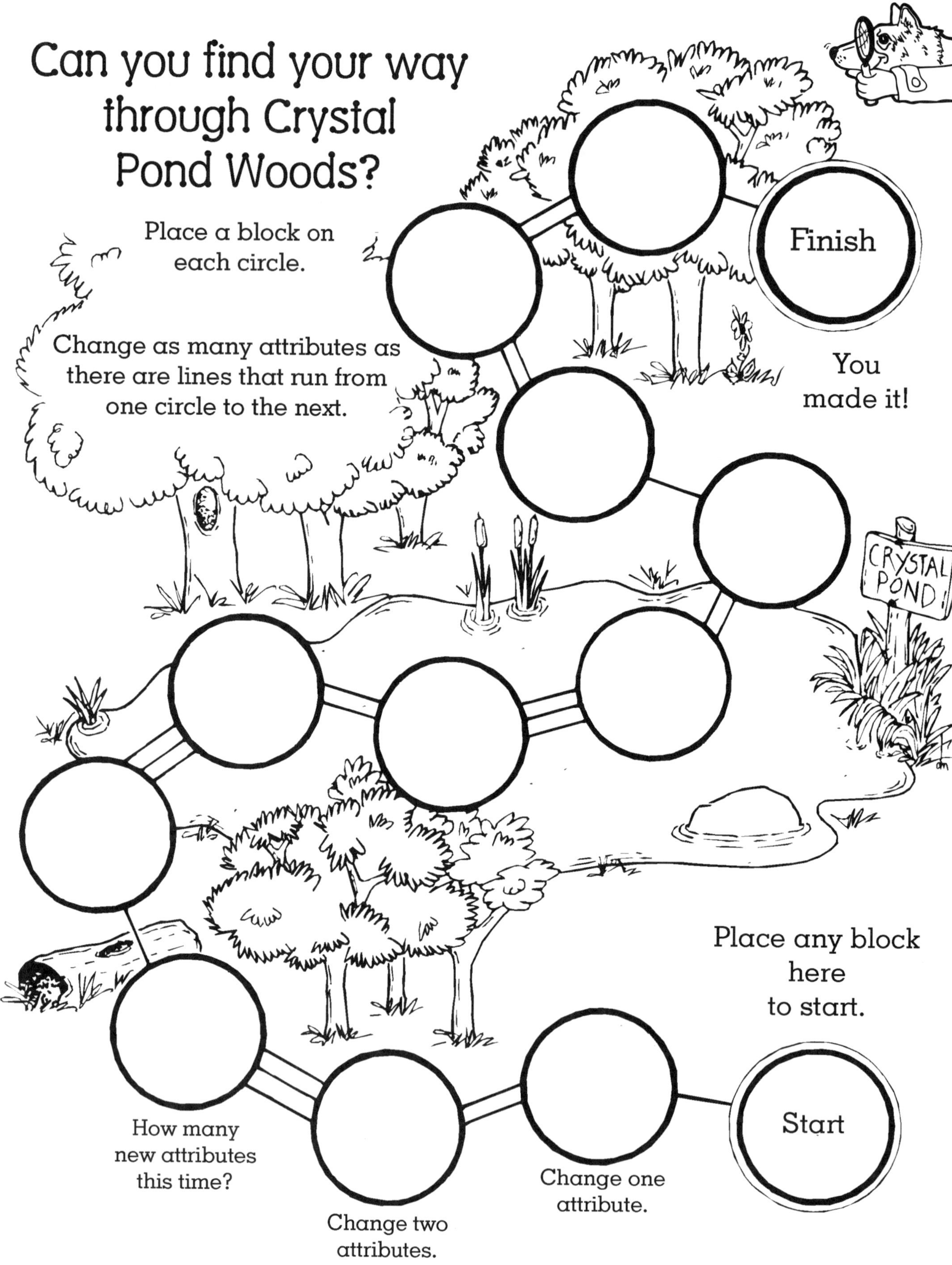

DETECTIVE THINKING
SMALL GROUP
LESSON 2

PURPOSE

The purpose of this lesson is to allow students to practice deductive thinking through the use of **Venn diagrams**. The teacher will give guided practice using Venn diagrams, followed by students working independently to demonstrate understanding.

TEACHER MATERIALS

For duplication:

- — *PETS™ Small Group Checklist* for each student
- — *The Birthday Present* story to read aloud

- — a class display of the dots that accompany *The Birthday Present*
- — a set of markers
- — one *Friendly Clues* game board and clue cards for each group
- — one *Dudley's Dog Bones* game board and clue cards for each group

LESSON PLAN

1. Read the story, *The Birthday Present,* and lead students through the process of using a Venn-style diagram. Draw *The Birthday Present* dots on large chart paper or use the projection copy of the dots. Add the corresponding loops as described in the story. An alternative is to provide students with a duplicated copy of the dots so they can add the corresponding loops themselves. Be careful to loop the dots as described so the story will work.

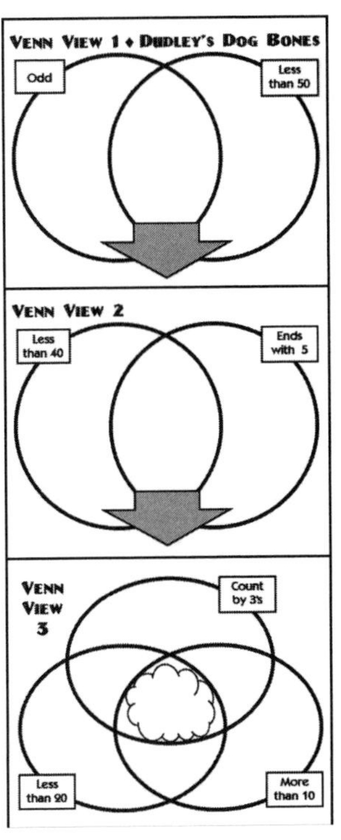

2. Prepare the *Friendly Clues* and *Dudley's Dog Bones* game boards and clue cards before starting the activity. While the two *Friendly Clues* boards may be run back-to-back, making one long *Dudley's Dog Bones* game board is recommended (as shown). Laminating these materials for use year after year is also recommended.

3. Give each group of students a *Friendly Clues* game board and set of the clue cards. After reading the animal names on the cards, have students place them in the correct sections of Venn View 1. When this has been done, use **ONLY** the cards in the

center intersection area of the Venn diagram to complete Venn View 2. Remove and discard all the other cards.

4. Give each group of students a *Dudley's Dog Bones* game board and set of tree clue cards. Have students place the trees in the correct sections of Venn View 1 (note that not all the trees can be placed in the Venn View). When this has been done, use only the trees in the center section to complete Venn View 2. When this has been done, use only those trees in the center section of Venn View 2 to complete Venn View 3.

ANSWER KEY

Friendly Clues frog

Dudley's Dog Bones tree #15

DIAGNOSTIC NOTES

Look for students who:

- — demonstrate a quick grasp of the concept of Venn diagrams by recognizing that each animal or number has only one correct space on the diagram.
- — see the overlapping attributes correctly.
- — leap intuitively to correct responses without manually working the entire diagram.

NOTES

The Birthday Present

Dudley the Detective loves to play games with his friends in Crystal Pond Woods. In fact, he loves them so much that he often makes up games to challenge his friends with mysteries. On a bright, clear Saturday morning, Dudley was going to a birthday party Sybil the Scientist was giving for Felix Frog. Many of Dudley's best friends would be there, including Rascal Raccoon, Yolanda the Yarnspinner, Rosalyn Robin, Isabel the Inventor, Max the Magician, and many other creatures from Crystal Pond Woods. Dudley was especially excited about going to this party because he was very proud of the game he had created for Felix Frog and his other friends to play during the celebration.

When Dudley reached Sybil's house, the party was just getting started. The friends played many party games, including "Hide the Acorn" and "Pin the Tail on the Tadpole." (Dudley secretly thought his game would be the most fun of all.) The friends ate cake, and then it was time for Felix Frog to open his presents. When the pile of presents was gone, Rosalyn Robin turned to Dudley. "You didn't bring a present for Felix!" she scolded.

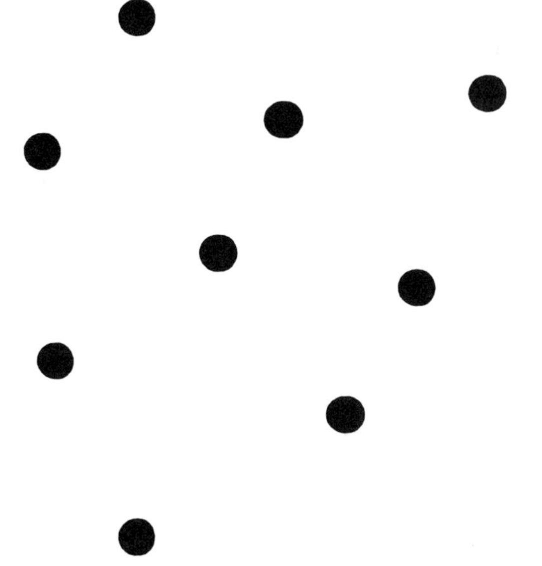

"Oh, yes, I did," Dudley replied. "I drew Felix a picture of himself."

"Oh boy, let me see it!" Felix exclaimed excitedly.

Dudley held out his picture for all to see. Felix Frog looked disappoint- ed. "I don't see myself," he said sadly. "It just looks like a bunch of black dots."

"That's because we have to play a game to find out which dot is you," Dudley replied.

Tommy Turtle squealed happily. "Is it a detective game?" he asked excitedly.

"Yes," smiled Dudley,"it is." He drew an orange ring around some of the dots on his picture.

"The dots inside the orange ring are all of us who hop along the ground," said Dudley.

"Oh," sighed Tommy. "Then I am not in your ring. With my heavy shell and short legs, I certainly do not hop."

"That's all right," said Yolanda. "Even with all my eight legs, I cannot hop. So my dot would not be in the ring either."

Rosalyn chirped happily. "I would be in the orange ring, because when I am not flying in the air, I hop along the ground to look for tasty worms and bugs. But Max, Sybil, and Felix would be in the orange ring, too, so I still do not know which dot is for me."

Dudley then drew a purple ring on the drawing. "Everyone inside the purple ring lays eggs," he said. "That is your second clue."

"Then I am outside of both rings," said Rascal. "I do not hop or lay eggs. But then, neither do you, Dudley, nor does Isabel."

"I do not lay eggs, and neither does Sybil," said Max. "But both kangaroos and rabbits hop, so these two dots must be for us."

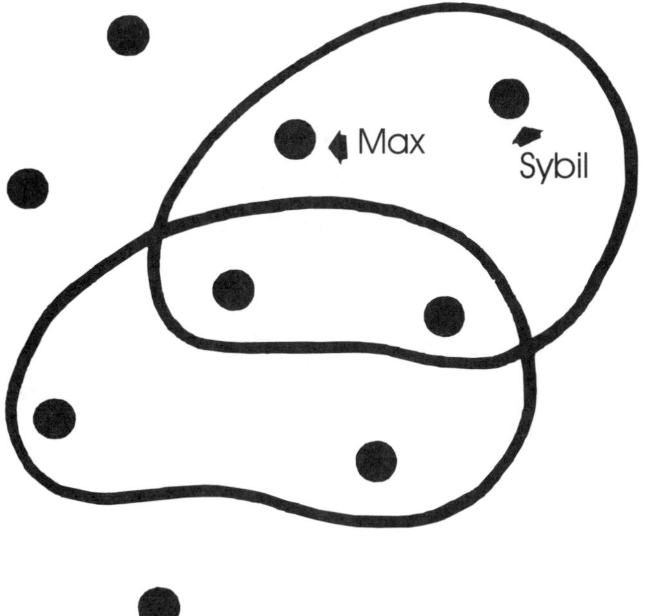

"That is correct. But what would Felix, the birthday guest of honor, be?" Dudley asked in a mysterious voice.

"Well," said Felix, "I hop along the ground, <u>and</u> frogs lay eggs. So I must be one of these dots in the purple ring and the orange ring, too."

"Very good," Dudley agreed.

"I would be in the purple ring," said Tommy. "Turtles lay eggs. Yolanda, you would be in the purple ring, too. But which of the dots is mine?"

Dudley smiled a mysterious smile and drew a green ring on his picture. "Now for your third clue," he said. "Everyone in the green ring hibernates through the winter."

"That certainly leaves me out," said Yolanda. "Spiders most certainly do not hibernate."

"Then I know which dot is you!" cried Tommy. "You are the dot who lays eggs, but does not hop or hibernate! I know which dot is me, too, and which dot is Rosalyn!"

CAN YOU FIND ROSALYN'S DOT AND TOMMY'S DOT?

Isabel cried out excitedly, "I know where my dot goes, too! My cousins, the tree squirrels, do not hibernate through the winter, but we ground squirrels do, so my dot would be here, with Rascal Raccoon."

"I know which dot is me, too!" shouted Felix happily. "I can even tell which dot belongs to you, Dudley! This was the best gift of all!" Felix cried. "Now I see that this IS a picture of me, and of you, too. This is a picture of my entire birthday party!"

The Birthday Present
The Answer

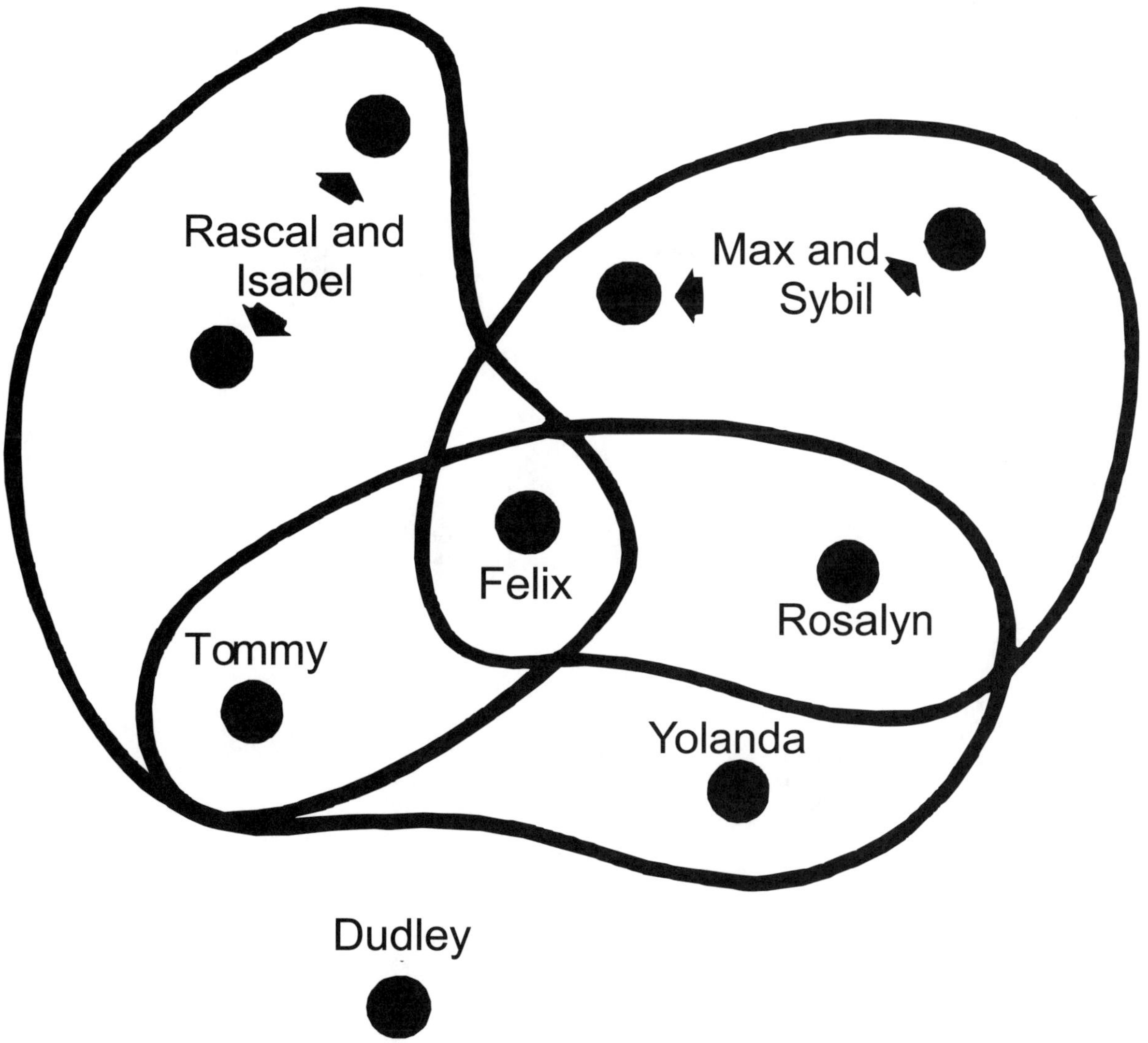

Rascal and Isabel

Max and Sybil

Felix

Rosalyn

Tommy

Yolanda

Dudley

The Birthday Present

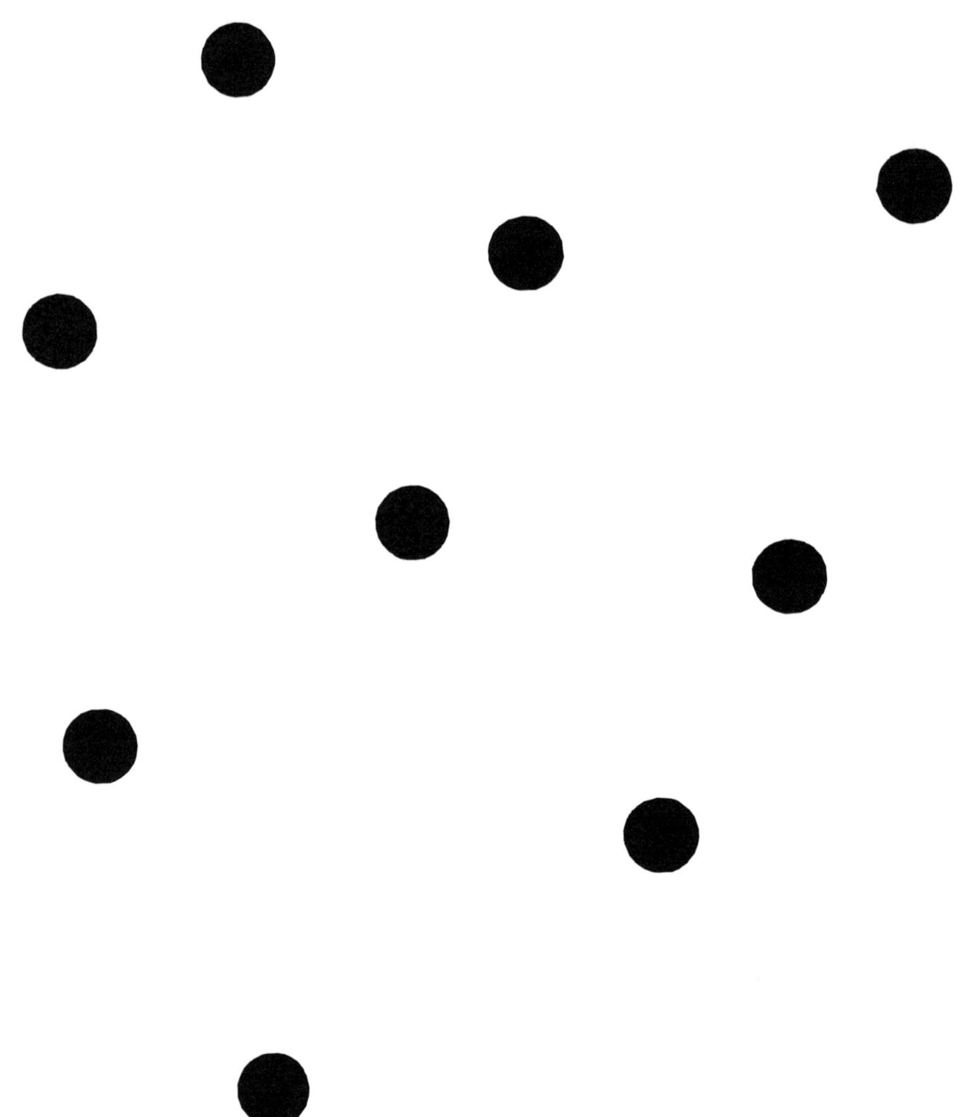

Can you find Felix's dot? Which belongs to Dudley?

Friendly Clues

Dudley the Detective is having some forest friends join him for his birthday party. One of his friends is bringing a surprise guest. Place the animal cards in the correct sections of Venn View 1 using Dudley's clues. Then move ONLY the cards from the center of Venn View 1 into the correct sections of Venn View 2.

Who is Dudley's surprise guest?

FISH	EAGLE	SQUIRREL
RACCOON	FOX	ROBIN
FROG	RABBIT	SNAKE
LIZARD	BEAR	FIREFLY
LADYBUG	CRAB	COYOTE

Venn View 1 • Friendly Clues

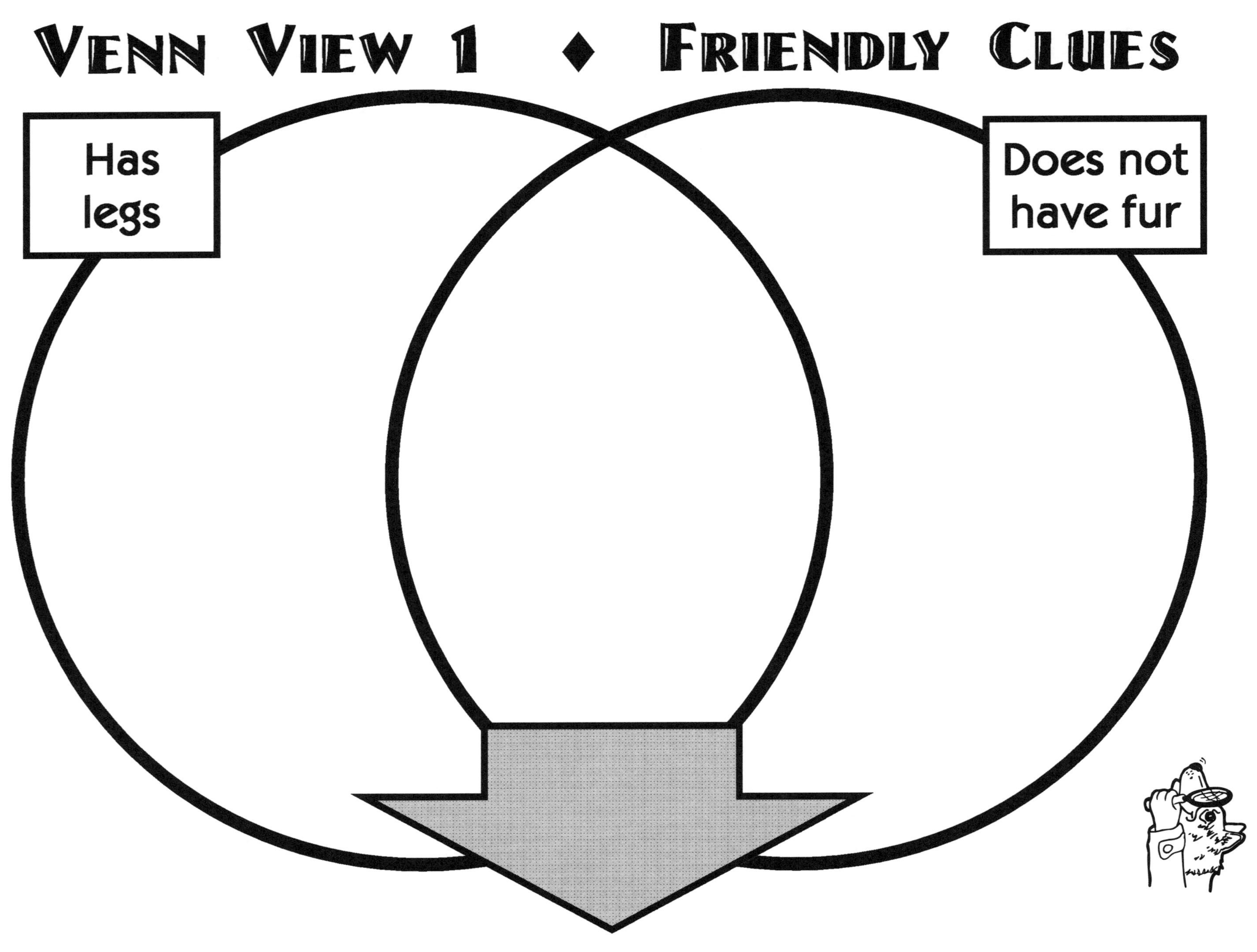

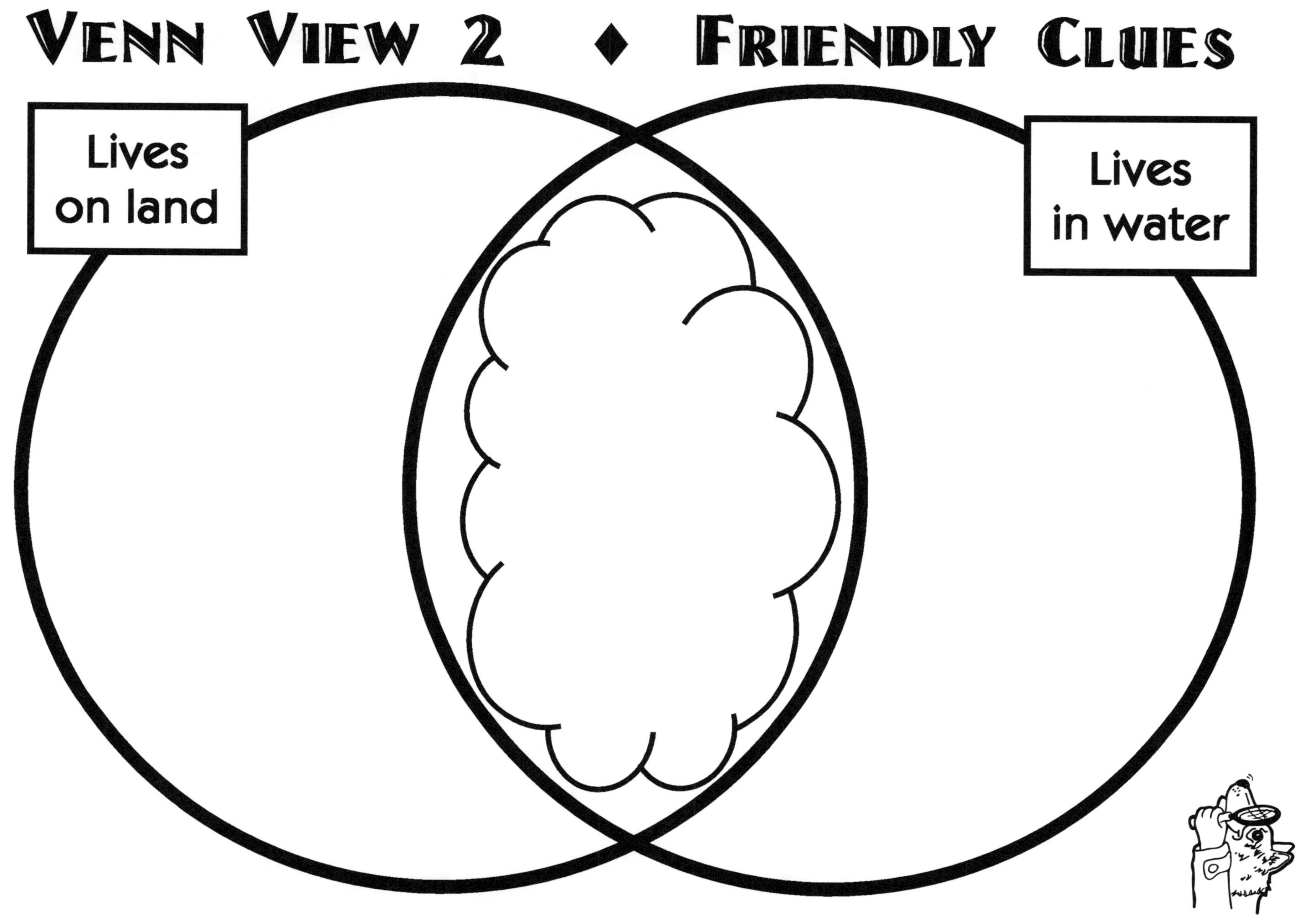
Venn View 2 • Friendly Clues
Lives on land
Lives in water

Dudley's Dog Bones

Dudley the Detective often buries his bones beneath the trees in Crystal Pond Woods. So he will not forget where he's hidden them, Dudley has numbered each tree in the woods. He has also drawn special Venn Views of Crystal Pond Woods that include clues to help him remember. Place the trees into the Venn Views using Dudley's clues. Under which numbered tree will Dudley's dog bones be found?

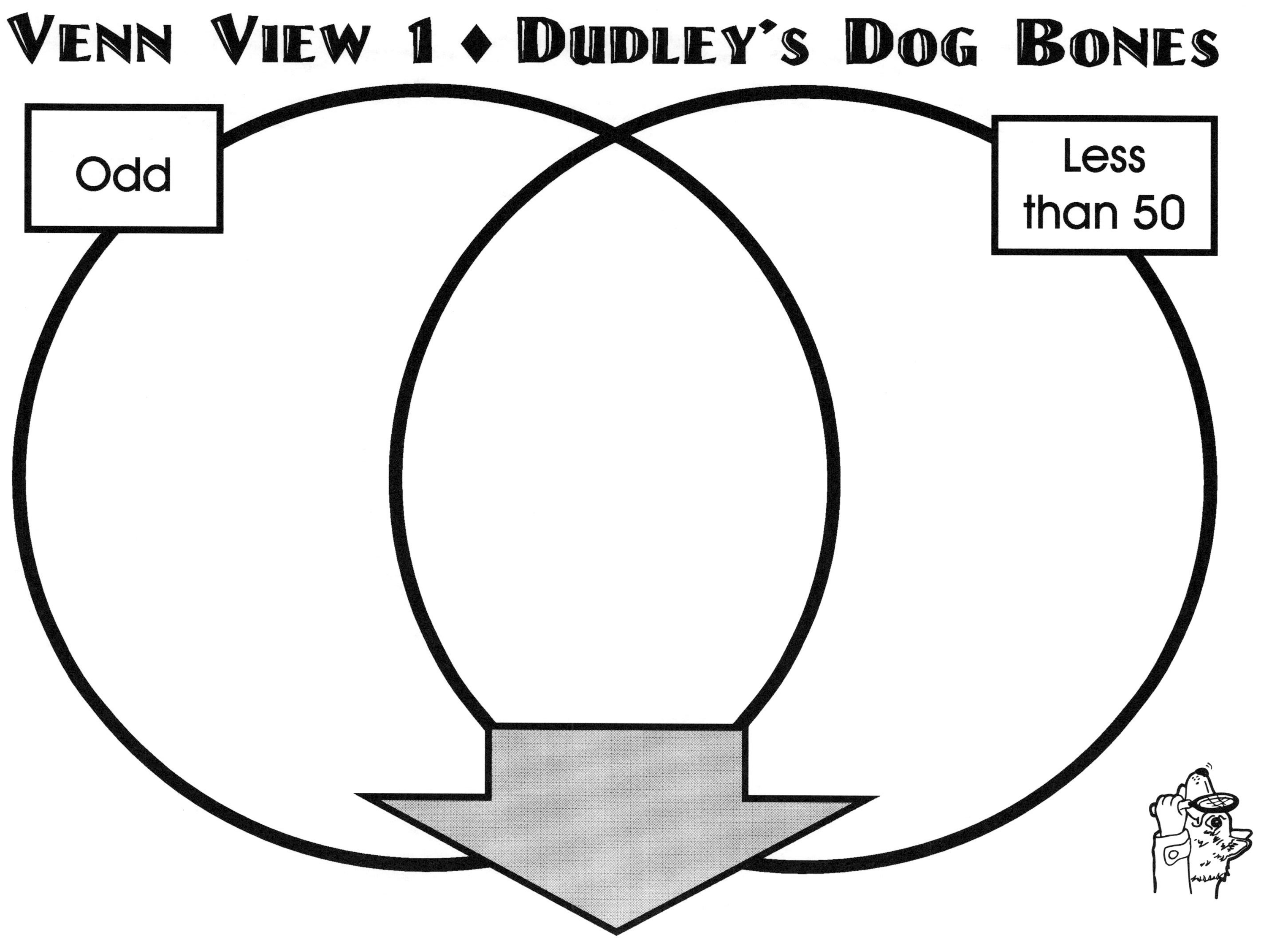
Venn View 1 ♦ Dudley's Dog Bones
Odd
Less than 50

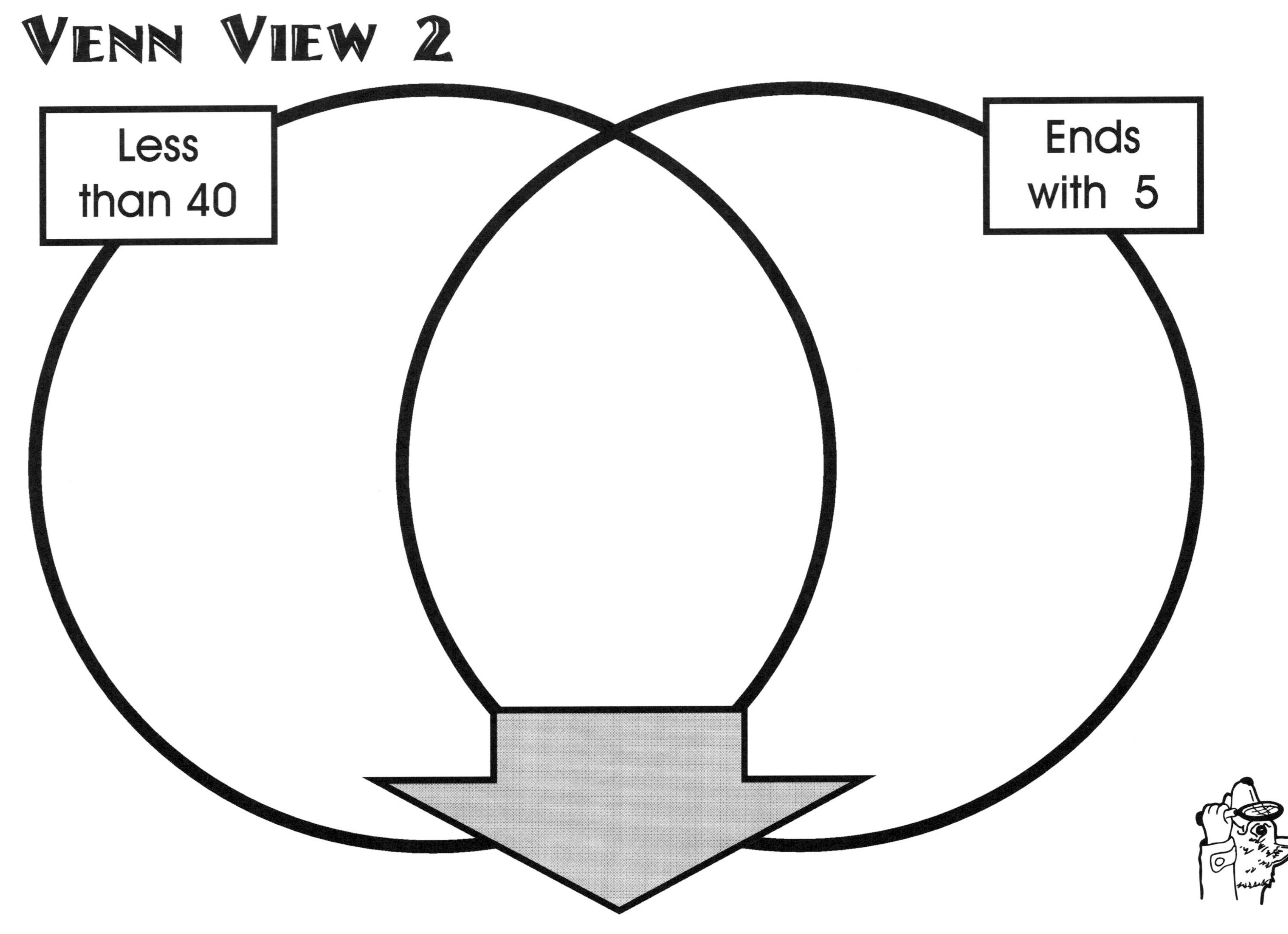
Venn View 2
Less than 40
Ends with 5

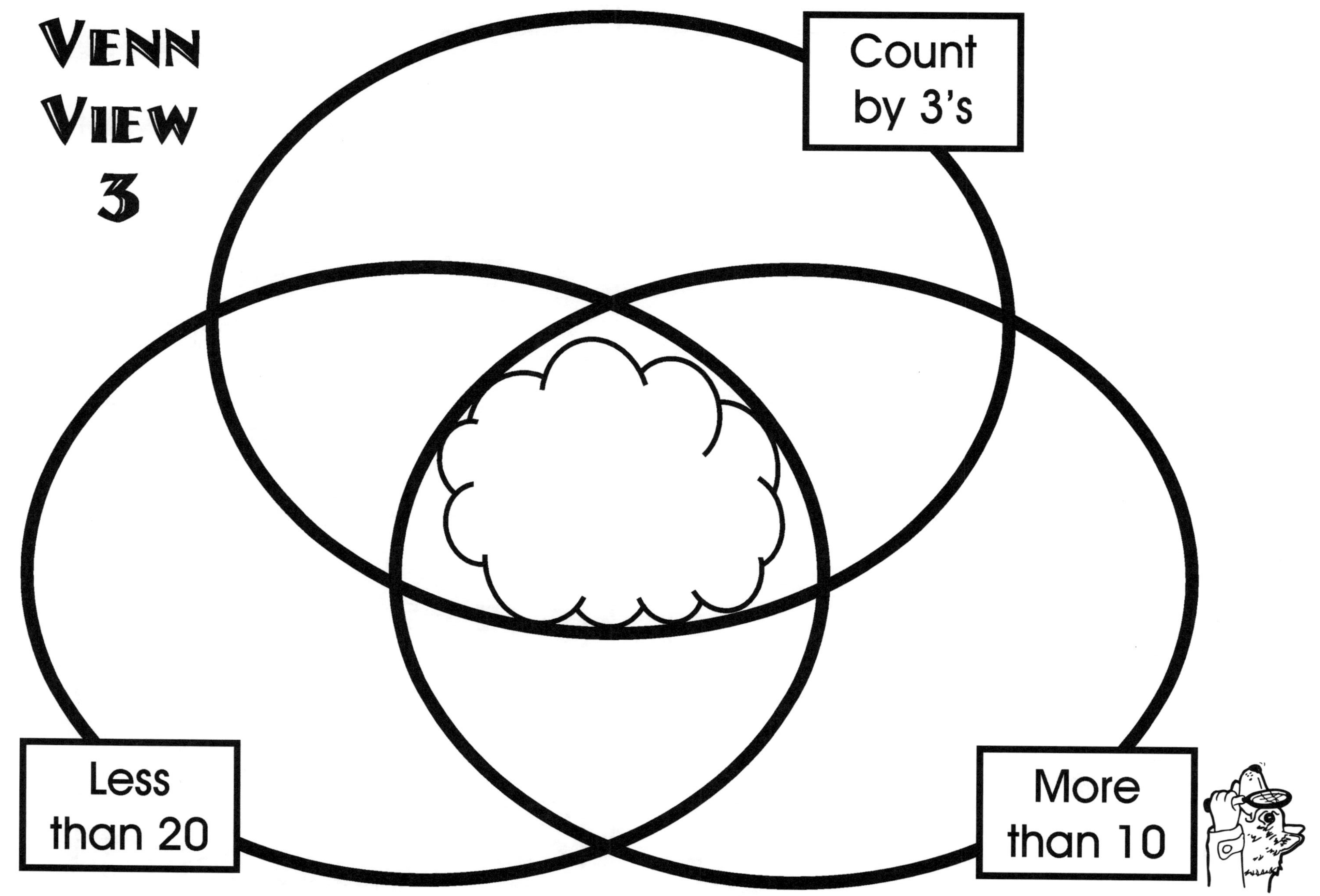
Venn View 3
Count by 3's
Less than 20
More than 10

Ask me what I did
in
Thinking Skills
today!
. . . using clues
to find
one, and only
one right
answer . . .
DETECTIVE
DUDLEY

Ask me what I did
in
Thinking Skills
today!
. . . using clues
to find
one, and only
one right
answer . . .
DETECTIVE
DUDLEY

Ask me what I did
in
Thinking Skills
today!
. . . using clues
to find
one, and only
one right
answer . . .
DETECTIVE
DUDLEY

Ask me what I did
in
Thinking Skills
today!
. . . using clues
to find
one, and only
one right
answer . . .
DETECTIVE
DUDLEY

Isabel

the

Inventor

. . . ***Brainstorms***

. . . To find

lots and lots

of answers

Divergent/Inventive Thinking

List names of students as each behavior appears. **Add checkmarks** after name if behavior is repeated. **Use a different color** of ink or pencil for each whole group lesson.	**PETS™** **Behavioral Checklist** **Inventor Thinking** (inventive/divergent thinking)	Teacher ______ Grade ______ Dates of whole group instruction: 1. ______ 2. ______

OFFERS MANY IDEAS (fluency)	**CHANGES COURSE** OF IDEAS; SEES **DIFFERENT PERSPECTIVES** (flexibility)
OFFERS OFF-BEAT AND/OR **UNIQUE IDEAS;** WORKS OUTSIDE CONVENTIONAL PARAMETERS (originality)	**ADDS LOTS OF DETAILS** OR **EXPANDS ON AN IDEA** (elaboration)
DISPLAYS UNUSUAL OR **MATURE SENSE OF HUMOR**	**USES ADVANCED VOCABULARY** IN A MATURE, ARTICULATE MANNER
RETAINS INFORMATION FROM PREVIOUS LESSONS	**PETS™ CLASSWORK** INDICATES AN OUTSTANDING ABILITY TO USE THIS THINKING SKILL

I see these behaviors in these students regularly during class time as well:	These students did not stand out during the PETS™ lessons, but I see these behaviors during regular class time:	Notes:

DIAGNOSTIC NOTES • INVENTOR THINKING

OFFERS MANY IDEAS (fluency) ♦ *generates many ideas* ♦ *all responses are acceptable* ♦ *responses do not have to be creative*	**CHANGES COURSE** OF IDEAS; SEES **DIFFERENT PERSPECTIVES** (flexibility) ♦ *offers different types of responses* ♦ *changes categories* ♦ *sees things from different points of view*
OFFERS OFF-BEAT AND/OR **UNIQUE IDEAS;** WORKS OUTSIDE CONVENTIONAL PARAMETERS (originality) ♦ *shares ideas that are very different* ♦ *reponds in ways that "stop you in your tracks"*	**ADDS LOTS OF DETAILS** OR **EXPANDS ON AN IDEA** (elaboration) ♦ *spends a long time adding details that may not occur to others* ♦ *piggybacks on the ideas of others*
DISPLAYS UNUSUAL OR **MATURE SENSE OF HUMOR** ♦ *understands your jokes* ♦ *makes jokes you appreciate*	**USES ADVANCED VOCABULARY** IN A MATURE, ARTICULATE MANNER ♦ *correctly uses words others do not know* ♦ *expresses ideas in a more mature, articulate manner*
RETAINS INFORMATION FROM PREVIOUS LESSONS ♦ *shares knowledge accurately during review* ♦ *applies knowledge during activities*	**PETS™ CLASSWORK** INDICATES AN OUTSTANDING ABILITY TO USE THIS THINKING SKILL ♦ *seatwork and/or challenge papers are exceptionally well done*

I see these behaviors in these students regularly during class time as well:	These students did not stand out during the PETS™ lessons, but I see these behaviors during regular class time:	Notes:
♦ *normally great inventive thinkers*	♦ *normally great inventive thinkers who "hid out" during the PETS™ lesson*	♦ *absentees* ♦ *new students*

- *be generous — more inclusive than exclusive*
- *names can go in more than one box per answer*
- *be sure to add ✓s after names for multiple answers*
- *be sure to use different colors for each whole group lesson*

INVENTOR THINKING
WHOLE CLASS
LESSON 1

PURPOSE

The purpose of this lesson is to introduce students to **divergent production** through inventive thinking. The students will be introduced to *Isabel the Inventor* who is able to see extraordinary possibilities in ordinary, everyday items. The lesson introduces the following concepts:

— When brainstorming, there are many acceptable responses.
— Seeing things creatively is important.
— Piggybacking on the ideas of others is to be encouraged.
— Impeding the free flow of brainstorming by expressing opinions about ideas is to be discouraged.

TEACHER MATERIALS

For projection:

— *Isabel the Inventor* picture – a colorized Isabel is available on the CD
— *Bubble Bonanza!*

For duplication:

— *Isabel the Inventor* story to read aloud
— *PETS™ Behavioral Checklist – Inventor Thinking*
— picture of Isabel the Inventor for each student to color
— class set of *Brainfocals™*
— class set of *Bubble Bonanza!*
— class set of *Yolanda's Cycle*

— a whisk (or any other utensil with holes may be substituted)

STUDENT MATERIALS

— crayons or colored pencils
— pencils
— scissors
— glue

LESSON PLAN

1. Introduce the lesson by asking students if they know what an *inventor* is. Brainstorm some inventors and their inventions. Be sure to include female inventors. Discuss with students what they think are some of the most important inventions. Point out to students that there is a difference between inventing something and discovering something. Students may try to suggest that Ben Franklin invented electricity. Franklin *discovered* electricity but did not *invent* it. A generator to produce electricity is an example of an invention. A discovery is something that already exists. An invention is a new idea or creation thought up by someone. The inventor is the first person to conceive the idea. The inventor may not actually make the object. Sometimes an inventor will hire someone else to make it.

2. Tell students that today they are going to meet *Isabel the Inventor* who thinks in a way that is different from her friends in Crystal Pond Woods. Project the picture of Isabel. Students may color their pictures of Isabel at this time or following the reading of the story.

3. Read the story, *Isabel the Inventor*. During the story, have students make their own special *Brainfocals™* to help them see things in new and different ways. *Brainfocals™* are the memory trigger for this unit. Copying the master for *Brainfocals™* on several brightly colored papers will provide students with the opportunity to mix and match colors. Students have the option of using the same shape and color or using different shapes and colors. Cutting out the pieces for *Brainfocals™* ahead of time will streamline this activity.

Brainfocals™ can also be made using die-cut shapes (like these award die-cuts with their centers punched out using another die) and a popsicle stick. Two die-cuts are pasted together and then pasted to a popsicle stick handle. Some die-cut systems even have an eyeglasses die.

Return to the story and have students brainstorm other uses for the whisk. Encourage students to think about changing the size of the whisk, imagining it to be larger or smaller. Be sure that the idea of using the whisk as a bubble blower is included.

4. Review with students these points from the story:
   - When thinking like an inventor, there are lots and lots of acceptable responses.
   - Looking at ordinary things in new and different ways is important.
   - Unusual and wacky ideas are welcome.
   - Piggybacking ideas is OK and should be encouraged.
   - Do not express opinions during brainstorming.

5. Introduce *Bubble Bonanza!* by having students put on their *Brainfocals™* and look at the bubbles. Ask students to think about all the possible things the bubbles could be.

Ask students to draw what they see when they look at the bubbles. Demonstrate with a smiley face how the circle should be incorporated into the designs and not become a frame for the designs. Do not offer further advice to the students. For example, if students connect two or more circles to create a design, it is more creative. However, it is NOT creative if the teacher suggests this beforehand. Refrain from guiding the students overmuch through this challenging activity.

Collect the *Bubble Bonanza!* worksheets when students are finished and score them. Suggestions for assessing student work are provided in **DIAGNOSTIC NOTES.**

CHALLENGE PAGE

Yolanda's Cycle

6. Distribute the challenge page which is to be done independently during class time. Read the instructions aloud, stressing the point that Yolanda has eight (8) legs. Encourage students to be as elaborate as they wish.

DIAGNOSTIC NOTES

According to the works of Frank Williams and E. Paul Torrance, creative divergent thinkers display fluency, flexibility, originality, and elaboration in their thinking. In addition, many researchers feel that another identifier of gifted thinking is an advanced sense of humor. During the whole class lesson, watch for students who have many unusual and creative ideas, who elaborate on their ideas, and who display enthusiasm for the activities.

A checklist for the whole class lessons is provided. The following is a short summary of student behaviors to note:

OFFERS MANY IDEAS (fluency) – All responses are acceptable. Look for students who generate many ideas.

CHANGES COURSE (flexibility) – This reflects a student's flexibility of thought. Note the students who truly see items in a variety of new ways.

OFFERS OFF-BEAT, ORIGINAL RESPONSES (originality) – Record the students with ideas that are very different. The ideas may be so wacky that they could not actually be implemented but the originality should be noted on the checklist.

ADDS LOTS OF DETAILS OR EXPANDS ON AN IDEA (elaboration) – Look for students who spend a long time adding details not considered by other students. Record here the students who piggyback on the ideas of other students.

DISPLAYS UNUSUAL OR MATURE SENSE OF HUMOR – Many talented students have an advanced sense of humor. Creative, divergent thinking activities provide opportunities for students to display this sense of humor.

USES ADVANCED VOCABULARY – These are the students who correctly use words classmates do not know. They sound very adult in the way in which they express themselves.

RETAINS INFORMATION – When reviewing ideas from earlier lessons, look for students who clearly recall the concepts and then effectively apply them to the current lesson's activities. While many children may grasp concepts "in the moment" of the instructional lesson, these students exhibit the significant ability to retain and apply new learning across time.

Bubble Bonanza!
This activity can be numerically scored to assess student creativity if the teacher wishes. Points may be awarded based on fluency, flexibility, originality, and elaboration. To score student pictures, use tally marks on the scoring grid at the bottom of the *Bubble Bonanza!* worksheet. Combine tally marks for a total creativity score.

Since each PETS™ activity is just one small piece of creating a whole-child picture of a capable learner, teachers should err on the side of inclusion rather than exclusion. More data gathered about each child is preferable to less data.

Scoring for fluency: Award one point for each completed picture. If two or more bubbles are combined into one drawing, score one point for each bubble involved.

Scoring for flexibility: Award one point for each new category depicted. *(A student who draws an animal, then an outer space planet, and then a toy would be awarded 3 points, one for each of these different categories).*

Scoring for originality: Scan all the worksheets from the group. Award one point for each idea found only on that worksheet. *(An example would be the student who made fingerprint when no one else did.)* Ideas that are similar yet different in at least one concept may be counted for both students. Combining bubbles takes extra creativity and daring. Award a point for each combined bubbles picture.

Scoring for elaboration: Award one point for each bubble in which lines or shapes that are significant to the picture have been drawn outside of the bubble. This does not include combined bubbles which have already been evaluated. Award one point for each drawing that includes minute detail.

Yolanda's Cycle
Look for students who display a creative or elaborate design. In order to use this challenge page as a diagnostic tool, students must have the opportunity to work on it independently while in class.

ISABEL THE INVENTOR

One day Yolanda the Yarnspinner discovered an object in Crystal Pond Woods that she had never seen before and did not know what it was. *(Show the class a whisk.)* Yolanda knows that when she wants to find out the correct name for an object, Dudley the Detective is the one to ask. She hopped on her cycle and rode over to Dudley's house. Dudley knew the object immediately.

"Yolanda," said Dudley, "this is a whisk. It is used in the kitchen to mix ingredients like eggs."

Yolanda was very impressed. However, since spiders never cook, she realized she did not need a whisk for mixing ingredients. Yet is was so unique that she did not want to throw it away. What else could she do with it? "I need to show this to my friend, Isabel," she thought to herself.

Isabel is an Inventor. She loves to think about things in **new and different ways** – to **brainstorm** lots and lots of unusual possibilities for everyday things! When her ideas begin to flow, there is no stopping her! Her workshop is in one of the tallest trees in the Woods and is stuffed from top to bottom with wonderful, interesting items including a huge pile of nuts. Isabel's favorite saying is, "I like to store as many nutty ideas as I do nuts!"

"Isabel," said Yolanda, when she arrived at her friend's workshop, "I found this in my house today and Dudley told me it is a whisk. You know I never have ingredients to mix since I never cook, but I still really like it. Can you help me figure out what else I can do with it?"

Isabel loves challenges and was excited to have a chance to do some brainstorming. "I'd love to brainstorm with you, Yolanda. Then you'll have **lots and lots of ideas**! All we have to do is look at this whisk in new and different ways. You can even add to, or **piggyback**, on any of my ideas!"

"I love to go for piggyback rides!" exclaimed Yolanda. "Let's begin!"

Isabel began to look at this whisk from all different angles. She considered a number of possibilities, like a drumstick or a rug beater, but none of them seemed very interesting.

"Wait, Yolanda!" Isabel called out. "I need my **Brainfocals™**! You've heard of **bi**focals that help people see, right? Well, Brainfocals™ are very special glasses that help focus my brain so I 'see' things in lots of new and different ways!" Isabel excitedly put on her Brainfocals™. Her eyes began to sparkle. Ideas flowed from her brain. "A tree ornament ... or a hanging plant holder ... a hair curler!" she exclaimed.

Yolanda could tell that Isabel was having a great time brainstorming new ideas. She wanted to try, too. Timidly, she shared, "This might not be a very good idea, but – "

"Wait, Yolanda!" Isabel stopped her. "During brainstorming, Yolanda, all ideas are accepted. We don't tell our feelings about ideas – we just say our ideas! The important thing is to get as many ideas as we can. Let's make a pair of Brainfocals™ for you, Yolanda, so your brain will see the whisk in new and different ways, too!"

Isabel helped Yolanda make a pair of Brainfocals™, and Yolanda began to add ideas to her list. Isabel and Yolanda were brainstorming some very unusual ideas.

(At this point, tell the students that they are going to make their own Brainfocals™, too. When they are done, brainstorm with students other possible uses for the whisk. Encourage unusual ideas, but accept all ideas. Include the idea of using the whisk as a bubble blower.)

Finally Isabel and Yolanda had filled up Yolanda's list with lots and lots of different kinds of ideas.

"Wow, Isabel," exclaimed Yolanda, "you are right about storing many nutty ideas. I love all our ideas! I think my favorite one, though, is to use the whisk to blow bubbles! We need to go find some bubble-blowing solution."

"Don't worry," Isabel replied. "I don't have any bubble- blowing solution, but I'll bet we can invent our own. Then we can go to the meadow and spend the afternoon blowing bubbles!"

Brainfocals™

Name:

Cut out the 2 arms and any 2 shapes.
Glue together and decorate.

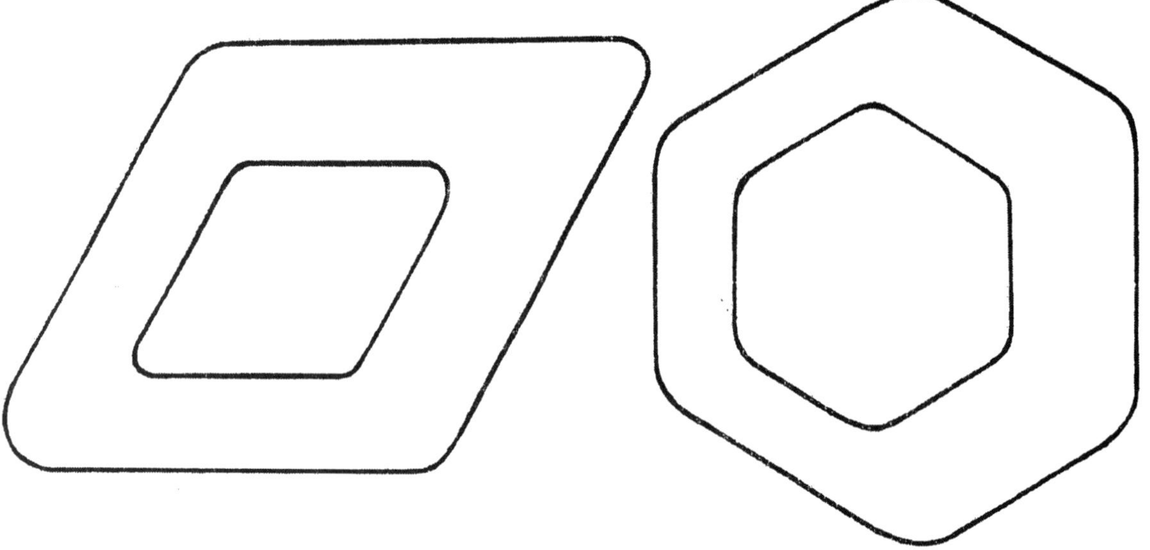

Name ______________________________

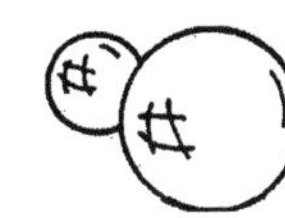

Bubble Bonanza!

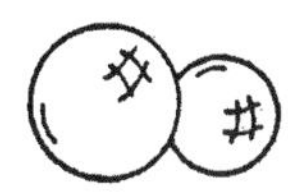

Using your Brainfocals™, look at Isabel's bubbles in new and different ways. Draw what you "see."

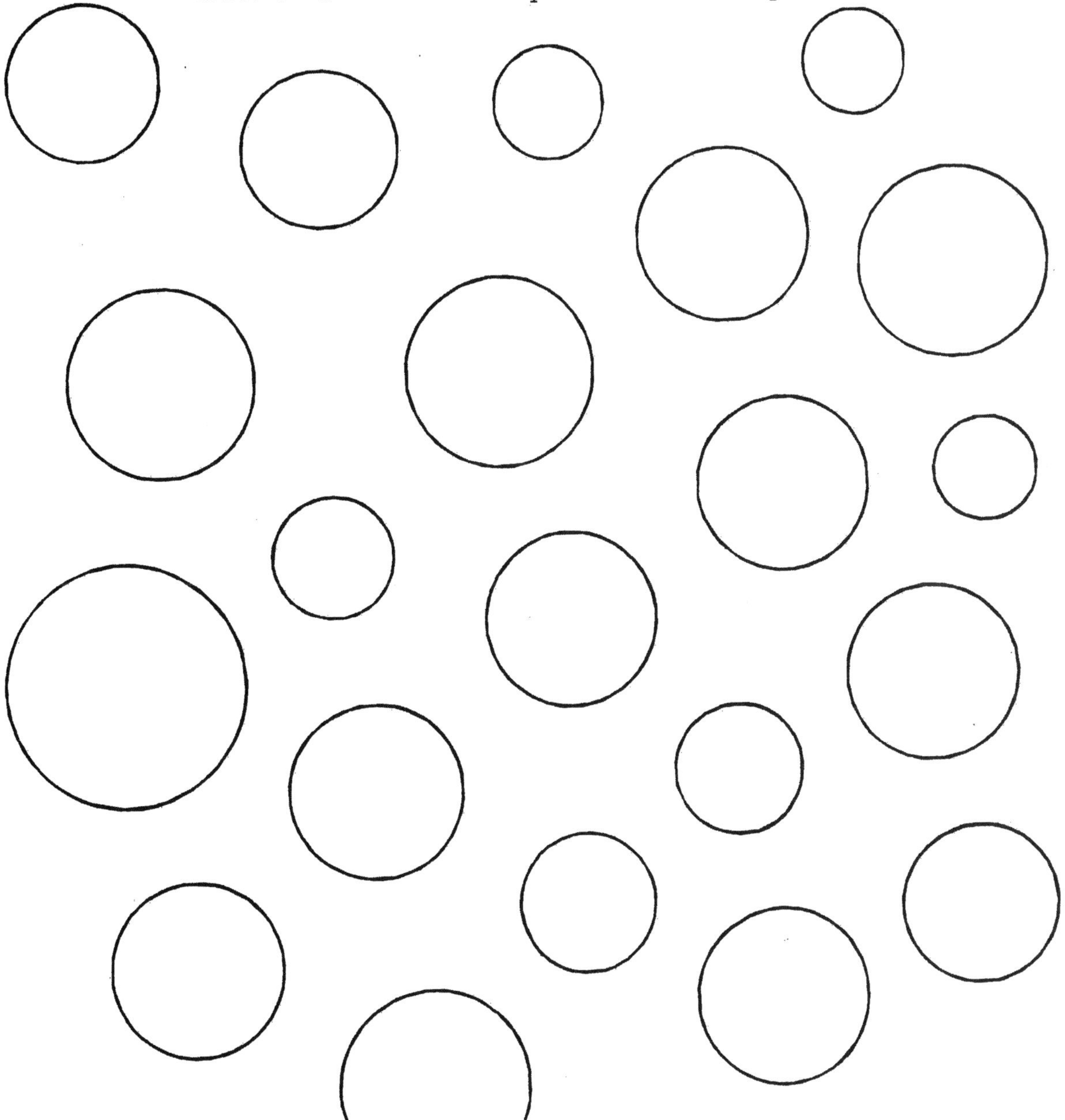

F	O
F	E

Name ____________________________________

Yolanda's Cycle

Your **bi**cycle has 2 wheels and 2 pedals. Help Isabel the Inventor design a new **spicycle** for her friend, Yolanda. Remember — Yolanda's a spider and has 8 legs!

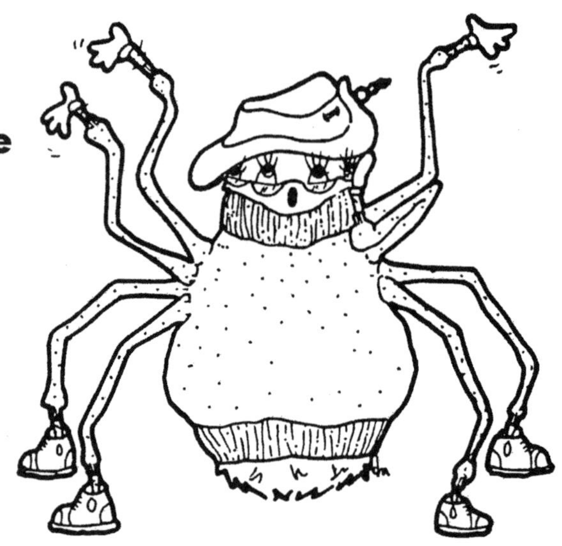

INVENTOR THINKING
WHOLE CLASS
LESSON 2

PURPOSE

The purpose of this lesson is to review and develop **divergent production of ideas** as inventive thinkers. The lesson extends and supports the concepts covered in Inventor Thinking Whole Class Lesson 1.

TEACHER MATERIALS

For duplication:

— *PETS™ Behavioral Checklist – Inventor Thinking*
— class set of *Some Spare Parts*
— class set of *The Great Acorn Collection and Storage Machine*

— a teaspoon or fork

STUDENT MATERIALS

— crayons or colored pencils
— pencils
— scissors
— glue
— tape

LESSON PLAN

1. Review the characteristics of inventive thinking:
   — When brainstorming, there are many acceptable responses.
   — Seeing things creatively is important.
   — Piggybacking on the ideas of others is to be encouraged.
   — Impeding the free flow of brainstorming by expressing opinions about ideas is to be discouraged.

2. Discuss with students that many times inventors are also *problem solvers.* An example of this is in the first automobiles that were designed and driven. The drivers were unable to see while it was raining, so a woman fixed the problem by inventing windshield wipers. Brainstorm with students other inventions that were the results of a problem that needed to be solved.

3. Brainstorm with the students many uses for a teaspoon or a dinner fork. Allow free brainstorming for several moments. Then encourage students to think about how they

might use many spoons (or forks) together or for what they might use a gigantic spoon (or fork) or a very tiny spoon (or fork).

CHALLENGE PAGE

The Great Acorn Collection and Storage Machine
Some Spare Parts

4. After the brainstorming session, students should start the challenge activity. *The Great Acorn Collection and Storage Machine* and *Some Spare Parts* provide students with an opportunity to create and design a new machine. The two pages of *The Great Acorn Collection and Storage Machine* should be copied on separate sheets, then taped or glued together to make one very tall tree. This provides students with ample space to use *Some Spare Parts* and their own additional drawn pieces to create a unique machine for collecting and storing nuts.

Explain that Isabel has a variety of things – spare parts – for students to use when creating their machines. Students must use at least two of the spare parts. They may use as many more of them as they like and may also include items or ideas of their own by drawing them. Some of the spare parts will not look familiar to students. Encourage them to think of uses for these parts despite the fact they may not know what they are.

Demonstrate to students how to use arrows to show movement that will clarify how their machines work. When they have finished creating their machines, encourage students to explain briefly how it works in the space beneath the tree. Let non-writing students dictate their explanations to an adult.

DIAGNOSTIC NOTES

This lesson provides additional opportunities for students to display the same characteristics emphasized in Inventor Thinking Whole Class Lesson 1. The following is a short summary of student behaviors to note:

OFFERS MANY IDEAS (fluency) – All responses are acceptable. Look for students who generate many ideas, especially those who continue to generate many ideas when shifting to the use of multiple spoons (or forks) or very large/tiny spoons (or forks) during the brainstorming session.

CHANGES COURSE (flexibility) – This reflects a student's flexibility of thought. Note the students who truly see items in a variety of new ways. They may use one of the spare parts in a way not usually intended.

OFFERS OFF-BEAT, ORIGINAL RESPONSES (originality) – Record the students with ideas that are very different. The ideas may be so wacky that they could not actually be implemented but the originality should be noted on the checklist. An example might be the student who uses the parts to build something three-dimensional. Also look for students who add very creative parts of their own.

ADDS MANY DETAILS OR EXPANDS ON AN IDEA (elaboration) – Note students who spend a long time adding details not considered by other students.

DISPLAYS UNUSUAL OR MATURE SENSE OF HUMOR – Many talented students have an advanced sense of humor. Creative, divergent thinking activities provide opportunities for students to display this sense of humor.

USES ADVANCED VOCABULARY – These are the students who correctly use words classmates do not know. They sound very adult in the way in which they express themselves.

RETAINS INFORMATION – When reviewing ideas from earlier lessons, look for students who clearly recall the concepts and then effectively apply them to the current lesson's activities. While many children may grasp concepts "in the moment" of the instructional lesson, these students exhibit the significant ability to retain and apply new learning across time.

The Great Acorn Collection and Storage Machine

When assessing *The Great Acorn Collection and Storage Machines,* look for the same behaviors noted for Inventor Thinking Whole Class Lesson 2. Elaboration and original ideas are the most easily assessed concepts.

NOTES

Here are a few spare parts from Isabel the Inventor's workshop. Use at least 2 of these parts to help Isabel move her acorns up into the hollow of her tall oak tree.

Some Spare Parts

Name ______________________________

Winter is coming. The acorns that Isabel eats during the long winter months are still scattered on the ground all over Crystal Pond Woods. She needs your help! Invent a machine to gather acorns and take them to Isabel's hollow near the top of this big tree. Draw and label your invention.

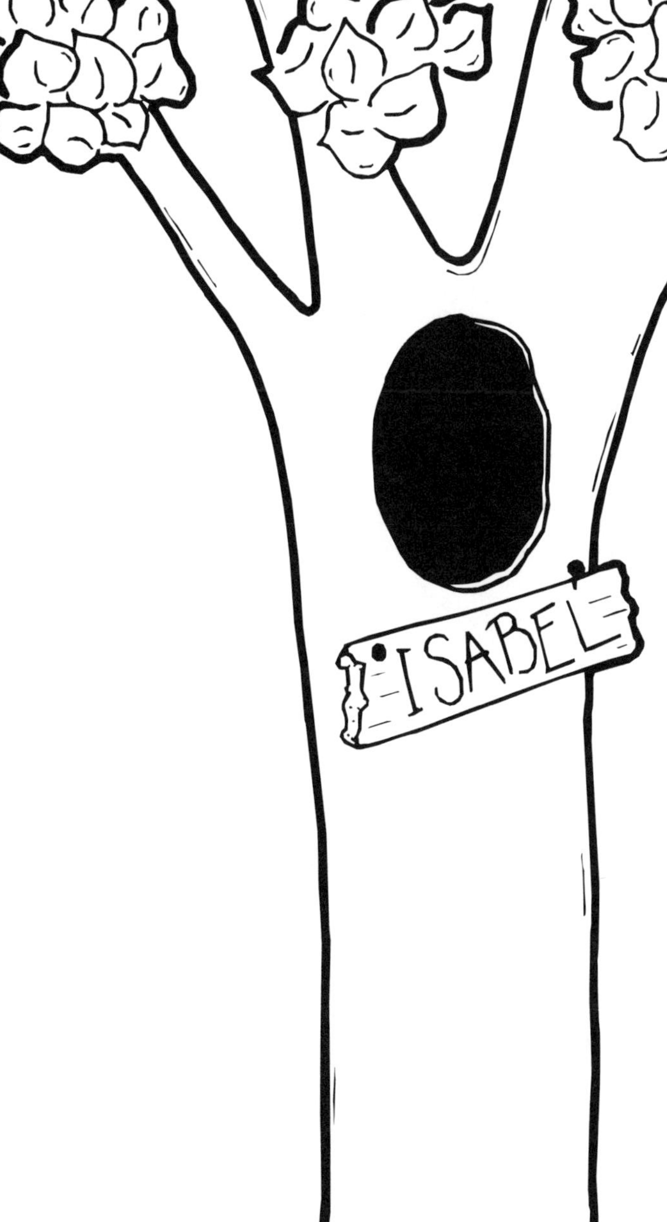

The Great Acorn Collection and Storage Machine

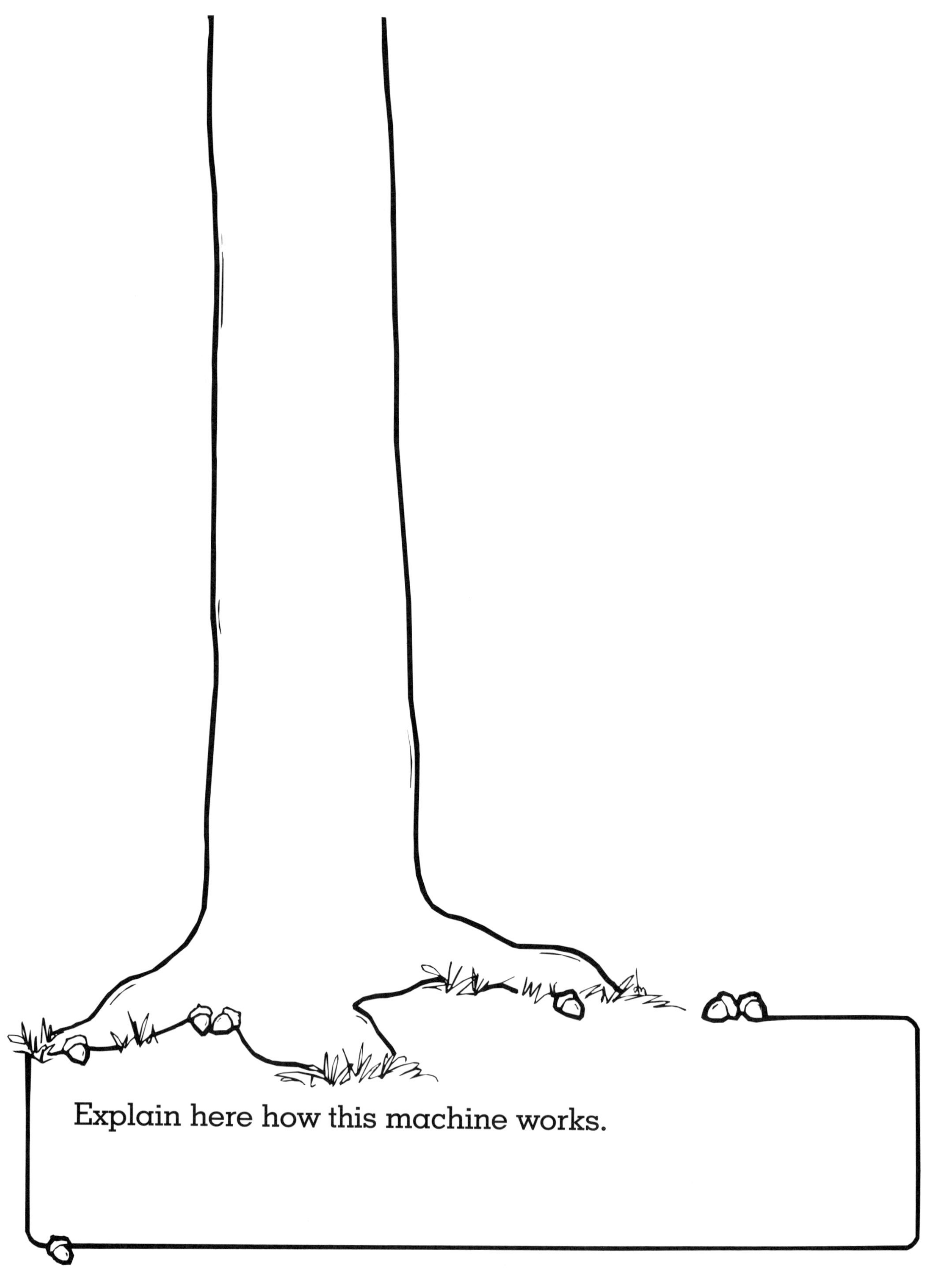
Explain here how this machine works.

INVENTOR THINKING
SMALL GROUP
LESSON 1

PURPOSE

The purpose of this lesson is to give students the opportunity to display their **divergent inventive thinking** by looking at shapes in new and different ways. This lesson showcases elaborative thinking as well as fluency, flexibility, and originality of thought..

TEACHER MATERIALS

For duplication:

— *PETS™ Small Group Checklist* for each student
— *Unique Ideas* for each student

STUDENT MATERIALS

— crayons or colored pencils
— pencils

LESSON PLAN

1. The following is a short story lead-in to the activity. It can be read to students or the directions can be given verbally.

Isabel found these parts of pictures hidden in the bottom of the big oak tree near Rascal Raccoon's home. She thought the pictures were very interesting, but they are not finished. After putting on her Brainfocals™, she saw many possibilities for finishing the pictures.

Directions: *Use your imagination to finish the pictures. Imagine what the pictures could be. Then add color and lines to finish them. Label them when you are done.*

2. Because elaboration (adding details) takes time, it is important to give students plenty of time. To ensure individual creativity, students should not sit next to each other. Do not offer advice to students. It is creative if students join pictures and draw outside the boxes. It would not be as creative if the teacher suggests this.

3. It may be necessary to ask students to describe their pictures and for the teacher to caption the pictures. This will help during the assessment of creativity.

DIAGNOSTIC NOTES

This activity can be numerically scored to assess student creativity if the teacher wishes. Points may be awarded based on fluency, flexibility, originality, and elaboration. To score student pictures, use tally marks on the scoring grid at the bottom of the *Unique Ideas* worksheet. Combine tally marks for a total creativity score.

Since each PETS™ activity is just one small piece of creating a whole-child picture of a capable learner, teachers should err on the side of inclusion rather than exclusion. More data gathered about each child is preferable to less data.

Scoring for fluency: Award one point for each completed picture. If two or more squares are combined into one drawing, score one point for each square involved.

Scoring for flexibility: Award one point for each new category depicted. *(An example would be when a student draws an animal, then an outer space picture, and then a landscape.)*

Scoring for originality: Scan all worksheets from the group. Award one point for each idea found only on that worksheet. *(An example would be the student who made the top right picture into a piano keyboard when no one else did.)* Ideas that are similar yet different in at least one concept may be counted for both students. Combining squares takes extra creativity and daring. Award a point for each combined squares picture.

Scoring for elaboration: Award one point for each square in which lines or shapes that are significant to the picture have been drawn outside of the box. This does not include combined squares which have already been evaluated. Award one point for each drawing that includes minute detail.

NOTES

Name ______________________________

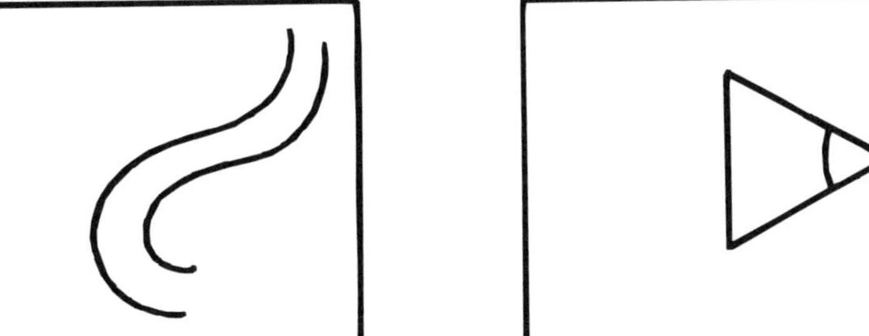

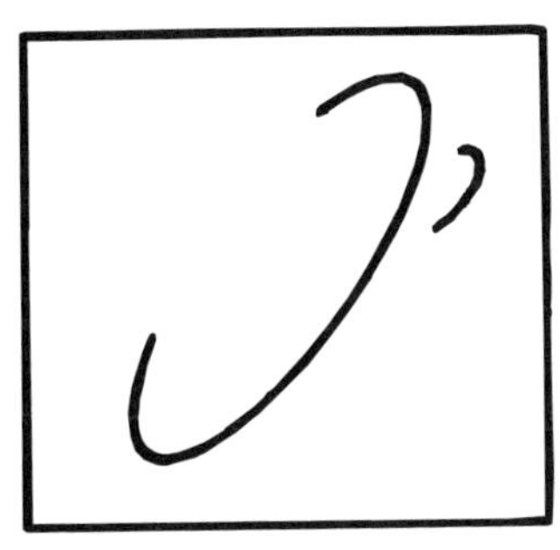

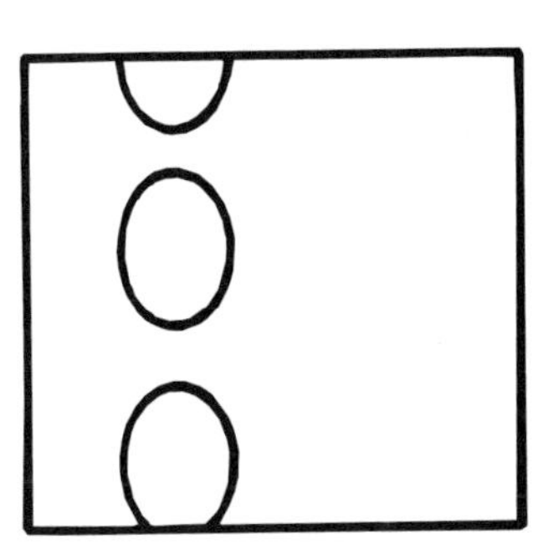

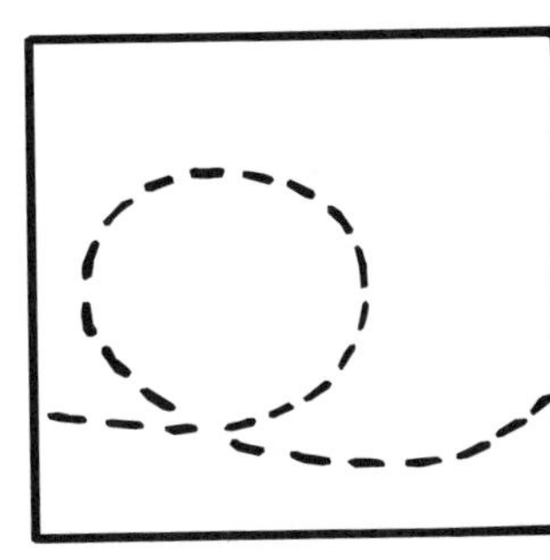

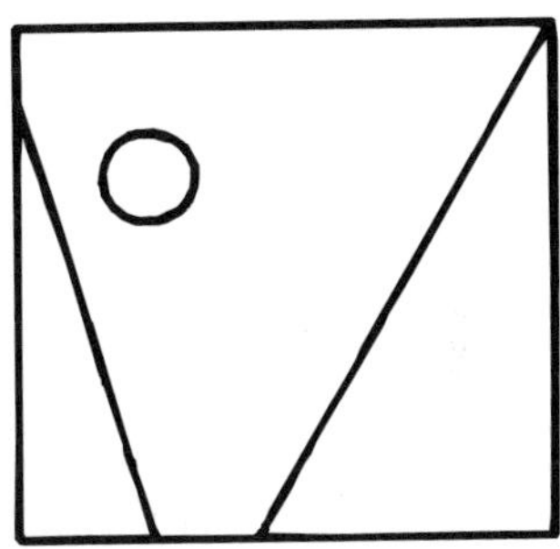

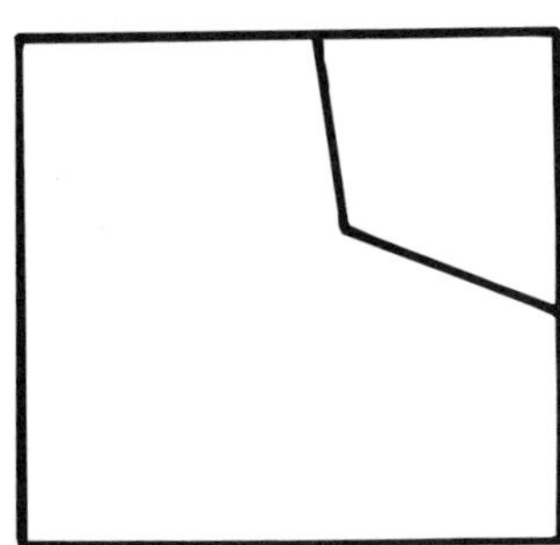

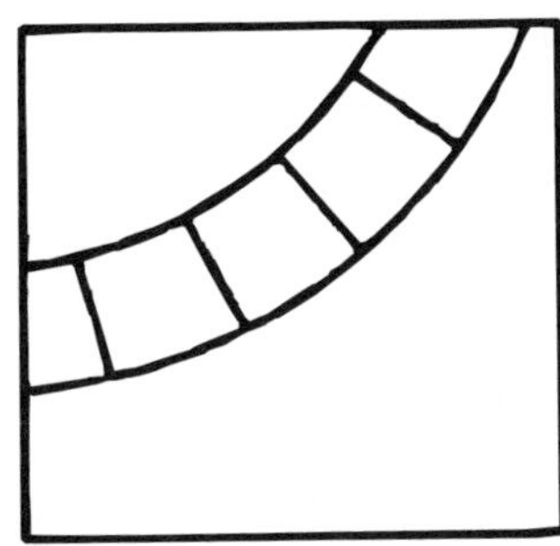

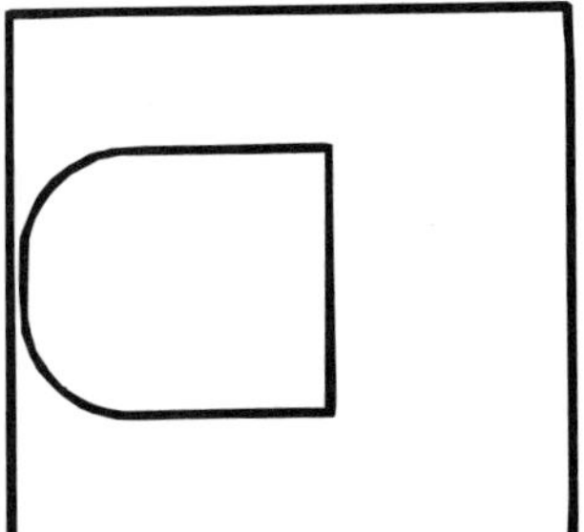

F	O
F	E

INVENTOR THINKING SMALL GROUP LESSON 2

PURPOSE

The purpose of this lesson is to allow students to practice their **divergent inventive thinking** by generating as many ways as possible to **combine** shapes with certain locations. In the small group setting and game situation, all students have to participate, even those who are not normally as vocal as their classmates. The teacher should encourage fluency, flexibility, and originality.

TEACHER MATERIALS

For duplication:

— *PETS™ Small Group Checklist* for each student

— game board *What Might This Be?*
— colored game pieces/markers to move around the game board
— beans or counters for keeping score
— a die
— one-minute timer
— a spinner for *What Might This Be?* (If a spinner is not available, number the six shapes on the game board from 1-6 and roll the die again instead.)

LESSON PLAN

1. Students are going to play the game *What Might This Be?* The four worksheets for the game board are provided and should be cut out and put together prior to the small group lesson. A copy of the spinner is also provided. A picture of how the completed game board should look is included. Students will need some type of game piece for moving around the board.

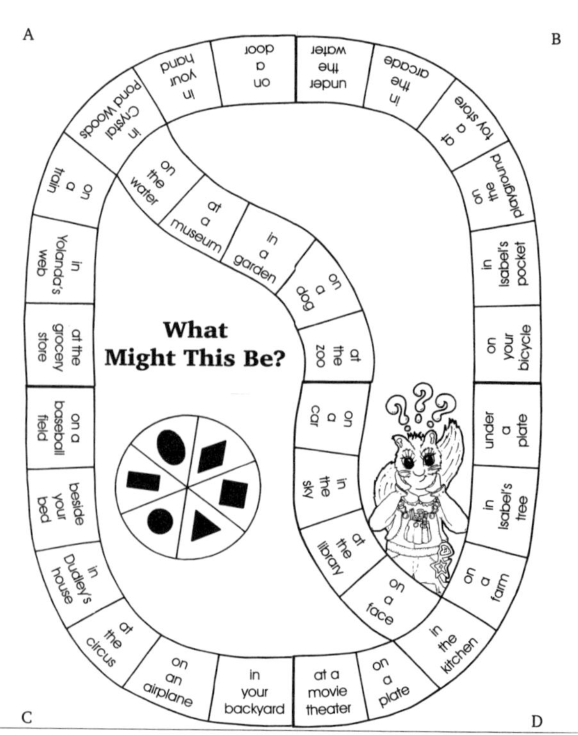

2. Instructions for *What Might This Be?*

— Each student places a game piece on a space of the game board path.

— On each turn, a student rolls the die and moves the appropriate number of spaces around the board. The direction a student's game piece moves around the board on each turn is determined by the player after the roll of the die.

— After moving his game piece, the student spins the spinner.

— Now the student must name something that fits the category created by combining the shape spun and the location of the game piece on the path. For example, if a student lands on a space marked "beside your bed" and spins an oval shape, the student must name something beside a bed that is oval-shaped.

— Level 1: Name one thing.

— Level 2: Name as many things as possible in one minute.

Optional methods of play:

— Each idea is worth one point or bean counter. Scoring should be more inclusive than exclusive so as not to stifle the flow of creative ideas.

— If the student whose turn it is runs out of ideas before the minute is up, that student can announce, "Group!" and then call on any of the other players. This approach minimizes blurting, maintains a creative flow, and redirects the group focus towards an overall group product from more competitive individual performances. For diagnostic purposes, the teacher keeps track of how many ideas the player whose turn it is initially produced.

With each round, students try to "beat" their best group score. When the session is over, tally all their ideas! Students are often amazed by how many ideas they can generate which encourages more successful brainstorming in the future.

— Role cards may be used to keep every student in the group engaged during each student's turn. After each turn, the cards and their respective responsibilities rotate so that each student gets a chance to do each job:

— The **Brainstormer** tells the Timer when to turn the timer and starts the brainstorming.

— The **Counter** takes out a bean for each new idea.

— The **Checker** makes sure that the Counter does not forget to take out a bean for each idea.

— The **Manager** makes sure that all is in order for a round to begin.

— The **Timer** is in charge of the minute timer. Only when signaled by the Brainstormer may the Timer start timing.

— If another job is needed, the **Cheerleader** is responsible for encouraging the group to come up with more ideas!

As students play the game, note students who:

- — offer creative, unique responses.
- — list a great many responses.
- — think flexibly, branching into new categories.
- — generate unique, original ideas.

DIAGNOSTIC NOTES

Here are some examples of creative responses given by students:

SPINNER	SPACE ON BOARD	RESPONSE
▮	on face	number one on a clock
▲	on a car	a car carrying home a Christmas tree
●	on the water	the reflection of the moon
●	in the sky	a Frisbee

NOTES

A

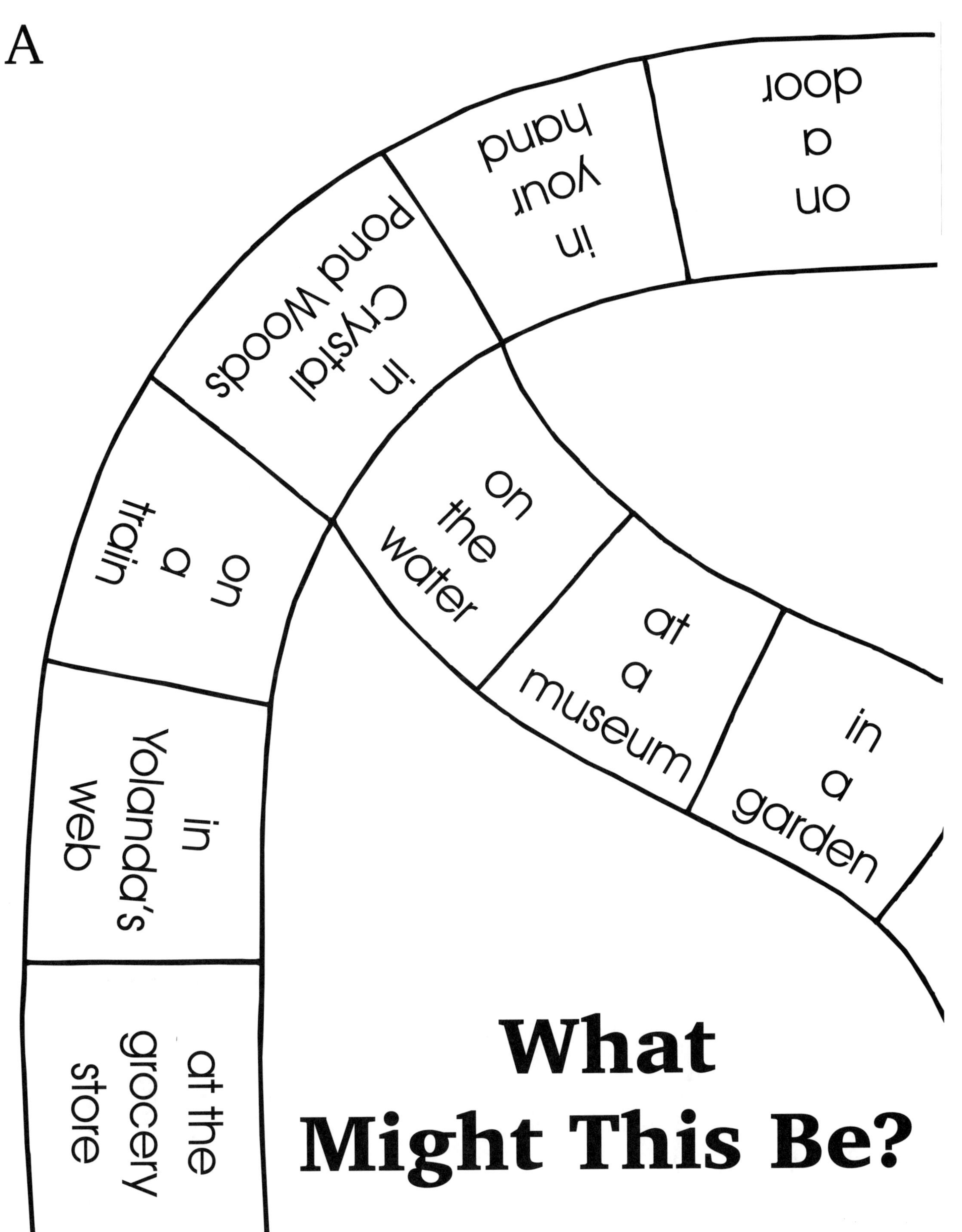

What Might This Be?

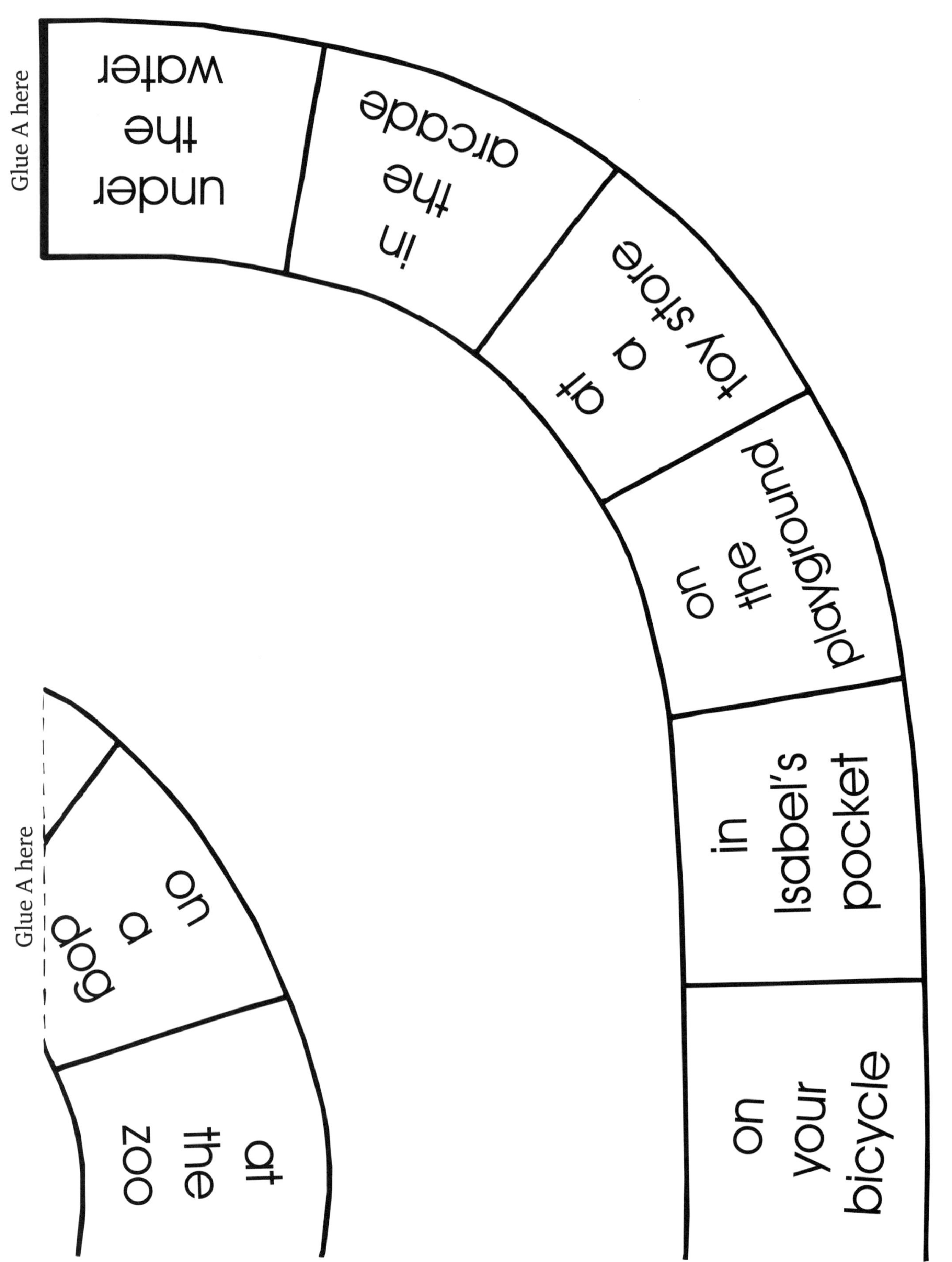
B
Glue A here
under the water
in the arcade
at a toy store
on the playground
in Isabel's pocket
on your bicycle
Glue A here
on a dog
at the zoo

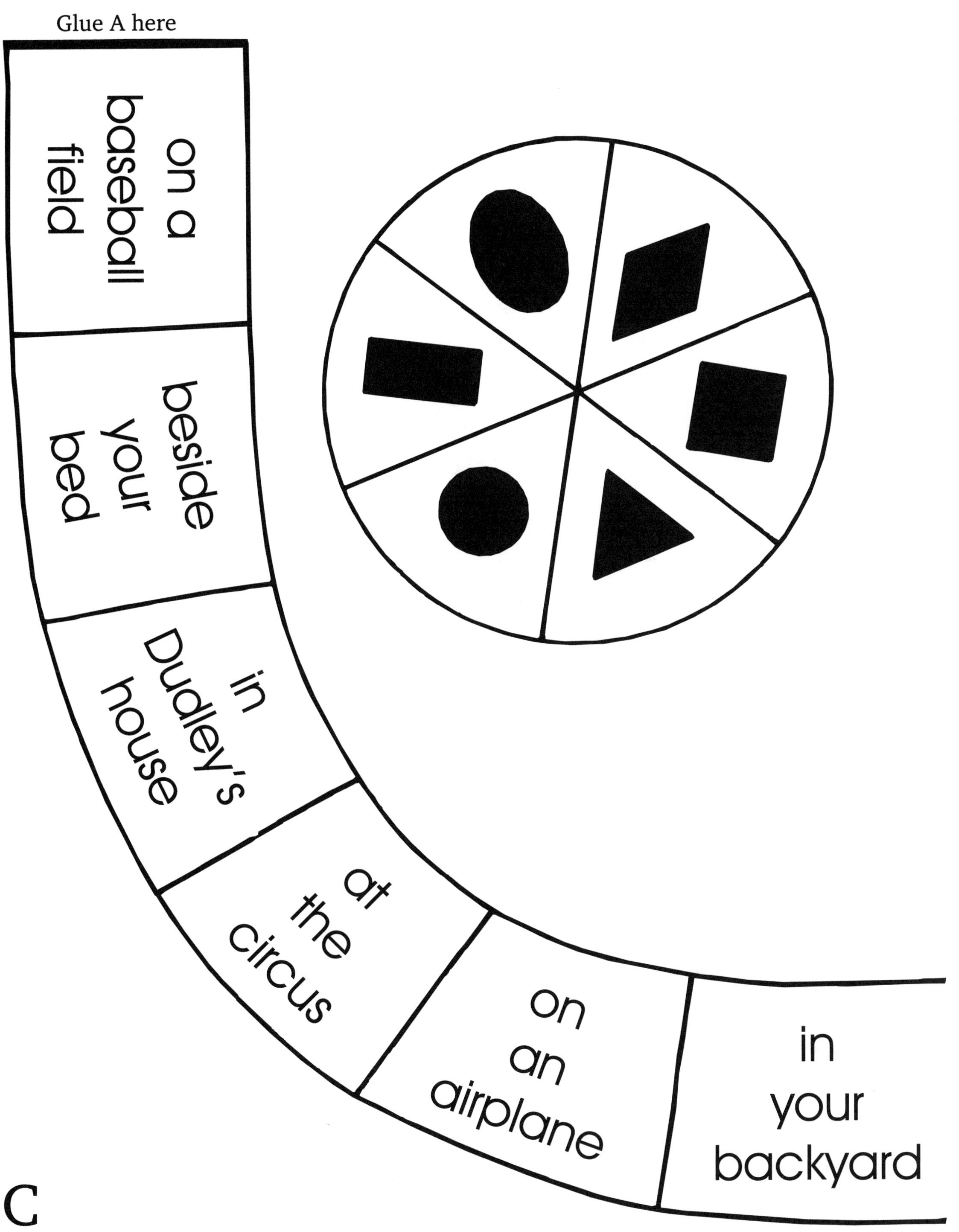
Glue A here
on a baseball field
beside your bed
in Dudley's house
at the circus
on an airplane
in your backyard
C

Glue B here

Glue B here

Glue C here

D

The Manager

Is everything under control?
Are we ready to start?

The Brainstormer

How many things are
that shape in that place?

The Checker

Watch the Counter.
Is it the right number of beans?

The Counter

Count one bean for each idea.

The Cheerleader

Good idea!
More ideas! Keep going!

The Timer

Take care of the timer.
Time's up!

Ask me what I did
in
Thinking Skills
today!
. . . brainstorming
lots and lots
of ideas . . .

Ask me what I did
in
Thinking Skills
today!
. . . brainstorming
lots and lots
of ideas . . .

Ask me what I did
in
Thinking Skills
today!
. . . brainstorming
lots and lots
of ideas . . .

Ask me what I did
in
Thinking Skills
today!
. . . brainstorming
lots and lots
of ideas . . .

Sybil the Scientist

. . . Studies

the parts

of things

. . . To

sort & classify

them

Convergent/Analytical Thinking

List names of students as each behavior appears. **Add checkmarks** after name if behavior is repeated. **Use a different color** of ink or pencil for each whole group lesson.	**PETS™** **Behavioral Checklist** **Scientist Thinking** (analytical/convergent thinking)	Teacher ________ Grade ______ Dates of whole group instruction: 1. _______ 2. _______

IDENTIFIES ATTRIBUTES ACCURATELY	**CREATES CLASSIFICATION SYSTEMS** THAT WORK
DEMONSTRATES UNIQUE STRATEGIES FOR ANALYZING	**DEFERS JUDGMENT;** GATHERS AND WEIGHS ALL DATA BEFORE DECIDING ON A SOLUTION
DRAWS RELATIONSHIPS BETWEEN LESSON AND OUTSIDE INFORMATION TO HELP DETERMINE SOLUTIONS	**RECOGNIZES FLAWED REASONING**
RETAINS INFORMATION FROM PREVIOUS LESSONS	**PETS™ CLASSWORK** INDICATES AN OUTSTANDING ABILITY TO USE THIS THINKING SKILL

I see these behaviors in these students regularly during class time as well:	These students did not stand out during the PETS™ lessons, but I see these behaviors during regular class time:	Notes:

DIAGNOSTIC NOTES • SCIENTIST THINKING

IDENTIFIES ATTRIBUTES ACCURATELY ♦ *recognizes and identifies attributes accurately*	**CREATES CLASSIFICATION SYSTEMS** THAT WORK ♦ *creates a classification system* ♦ *tries unique sorting approaches*
DEMONSTRATES UNIQUE STRATEGIES FOR ANALYZING ♦ *categorizes or sorts in unusual or different ways*	**DEFERS JUDGMENT;** GATHERS AND WEIGHS ALL DATA BEFORE DECIDING ON A SOLUTION ♦ *waits until enough information is gathered to develop an effective sorting system* ♦ *avoids guessing impulsively*
DRAWS RELATIONSHIPS BETWEEN LESSON AND OUTSIDE INFORMATION TO HELP DETERMINE SOLUTIONS ♦ *makes connections between activities and outside information* ♦ *applies the information*	**RECOGNIZES FLAWED REASONING** ♦ *points out errors in an effective sorting approach*
RETAINS INFORMATION FROM PREVIOUS LESSONS ♦ *shares knowledge accurately during review* ♦ *applies knowledge during activities*	**PETS™ CLASSWORK** INDICATES AN OUTSTANDING ABILITY TO USE THIS THINKING SKILL ♦ *seatwork and/or challenge papers are exceptionally well done*

I see these behaviors in these students regularly during class time as well: ♦ *normally great analytical thinkers*	These students did not stand out during the PETS™ lessons, but I see these behaviors during regular class time: ♦ *normally great analytical thinkers who "hid out" during the PETS™ lesson*	Notes: ♦ *absentees* ♦ *new students*

- *be generous — more inclusive than exclusive*
- *names can go in more than one box per answer*
- *be sure to add ✓s after names for multiple answers*
- *be sure to use different colors for each whole group lesson*

SCIENTIST THINKING
WHOLE CLASS
LESSON 1

PURPOSE

The purpose of this lesson is to introduce the students to **analytical convergent thinking**. They will meet Sybil, a scientist who loves to classify and organize the information she collects. The students will learn that in analytical thinking:

— There are no pre-determined rules for classifying. The scientist must classify data that has never been sorted and organized before, and it is up to her to determine the rules for sorting.

— There may be more than one equally accurate way to sort data.

TEACHER MATERIALS

For projection:

— *Sybil the Scientist* picture – a colorized Sybil is available on the CD

— *Sybil's Creatures.* The creatures should be colored and cut out so they can be moved around easily. Use a variety of colors and color some creatures with two or more different colors. A colorized version is on the CD.

— *Sybil's Laboratory*

For duplication:

— *Sybil the Scientist* story to read aloud

— *PETS™ Behavioral Checklist – Scientist Thinking*

— picture of Sybil the Scientist for each student to color

— class set of *Sybil's Magnifying Glass* (Inexpensive magnifying glasses can be purchased through novelty companies. Alternately, some die-cut systems have a magnifying glass die.)

— class set of *Loose Laboratory Limpets*

— class set of *Sybil's Laboratory*

STUDENT MATERIALS

— pencils

— scissors

— glue

LESSON PLAN

1. Introduce the lesson by asking students if they know what a *scientist* does. Discuss scientists and any real-life scientists known to students. Brainstorm the different kinds of things a scientist might study.

2. Introduce *Sybil the Scientist* to the students. Project the picture of Sybil who is wearing a laboratory coat to protect her from spills in her lab. In her many pockets, Sybil keeps her most important tools and materials. During the reading of the story, there is a

place to discuss with students the items in her pockets. Students may color their pictures of Sybil at this time or following the reading of the story.

Sybil is special because she thinks in a scientific way. Observations are very important to a scientist. Sybil uses all of her senses: tasting, seeing, hearing, smelling, and touching. Many scientists use a magnifying glass for more detailed observations of objects when they are collecting their data. After a lot of new data has been collected, a scientist like Sybil will organize or group the data. A more scientific name for "group the data" is *classify.* Scientists often read how other scientists classify data because there can be more than one way to organize it.

3. Read the *Sybil the Scientist* story into which is incorporated the whole class activity. During the story, students will be given actual magnifying glasses or will make *Sybil's Magnifying Glass*, the memory trigger for this unit. Towards the end of the story, project *Sybil's Laboratory* so students can make their own observations to classify the laboratory creatures.

In making their observations, have students focus on and discuss the different characteristics, or *attributes,* of Sybil's creatures. What are their characteristics? How are they alike? How are they different? Remind students that their observations need to be as accurate as possible.

When classifying the laboratory creatures into the four cages, it is important to accept any characteristic that makes sense. As students offer suggestions about how to classify the creatures, point out that the suggestions are called *hypotheses,* or educated guesses. It is normal for a scientist's hypothesis to change frequently. It is also quite possible that the class may not discover a workable hypothesis. That is part of science.

4. Review with students these points from the story:
   - When scientists receive new information, they organize it in categories or groups that have common characteristics.
   - Scientists group or classify the new information based on observations.
   - When classifying new information, there are no set rules. Hypotheses will change and evolve as they are tested.

CHALLENGE PAGES

Loose Laboratory Limpets *Sybil's Laboratory*

5. Distribute the challenge pages which are to be done independently in class. When giving the directions to students for *Loose Laboratory Limpets,* instruct students NOT to color the limpets. Decisions based on categorizing the limpets should take into account that the limpets are black and white. Students should glue their limpets onto the *Sybil's Laboratory* worksheet but only <u>after</u> they know what their classification system will be.

ANSWER KEY

The following are some of the possible ways *Loose Laboratory Limpets* can be categorized:

1. dots	2. cow spots	3. stripes	4. 6 or more legs
1. smiling	2. open mouth	3. sad	4. straight/squiggly mouth
1. 3 legs	2. 4 legs	3. 2 or less legs	4. plain

DIAGNOSTIC NOTES

Look for students who accurately sort the samples into discrete sets so that each group has at least one item but no item fits equally well into more than one group. Strong analytical thinkers may sort the data in more than one way, each time applying an equally good set of classifiers.

A checklist for the whole class lesson is provided. The following is a short summary of student behaviors to note:

IDENTIFIES ATTRIBUTES – Look for students who understand the concept of attributes (or characteristics) and identify them accurately.

CREATES CLASSIFICATION SYSTEMS – Look for students who create a viable, discrete classification system. They understand that a creature that is blue and white cannot be categorized in the blue *and* in the white categories. Also note students who try a sorting system that is unique, even though it may not work. Willingness to try something uniquely different is a trait of talented learners.

DEMONSTRATES UNIQUE STRATEGIES – Look for students who categorize or sort in an unusual or different way. They often change course and come up with ideas that other students have not considered.

DEFERS JUDGMENT – Look for students who wait before offering an answer, carefully weighing various options. These students may also think of ideas for a sorting system after the class has gone ahead.

DRAWS RELATIONSHIPS – Look for students who know or want to know specific facts about the world around them. Some students will bring a vast array of knowledge to class with them. This in itself does not indicate a talented student, but combining this with some of the other characteristics will give the teacher a more thorough picture of the student's potential.

RECOGNIZES FLAWED REASONING – Some students will focus on one characteristic and not give up, even when it's obvious that sorting by that characteristic will not work. Look for students who recognize when a certain sorting system will not work, particularly when they can explain why.

RETAINS INFORMATION – When reviewing ideas from earlier lessons, look for students who clearly recall the concepts and then effectively apply them to the current lesson's activities. While many children may grasp concepts "in the moment" of the instructional lesson, these students exhibit the significant ability to retain and apply new learning across time.

Loose Laboratory Limpets and ***Sybil's Laboratory***

Look for students who:

– accurately sort all the limpets into four discrete sets.

NOTES

SYBIL THE SCIENTIST

It was a beautiful day in Crystal Pond Woods. The animals were outside enjoying the great weather and preparing for the annual Crystal Pond Picnic. All of the animals, that is, except for Sybil the Scientist.

A scientist is a very special person. One of the things a scientist does is make careful observations of the world around her. **Observation** is a fancy word for looking at things. But a scientist does not just look at things. Sybil uses all five senses: seeing, hearing, smelling, touching, and sometimes tasting. She carefully records this information, which she calls **data,** in her journal. As Sybil collects data or new information, she tries to **organize or categorize** the information according to **rules.**

Sybil wears a white laboratory coat to protect her from possible spills in the laboratory. Her laboratory coat has many pockets filled with her most important objects. One of the objects she always carries with her is a magnifying glass. The magnifying glass allows Sybil to observe objects more closely. What are some of the other objects Sybil carries? Can you think of some reasons why Sybil carries these items in her pockets?

(At this point, engage the students in a discussion regarding the possible uses of the instruments. The books are especially important to scientists because they often read to learn more about the things that interest them. Scientists also read what other scientists are doing so they can compare data. The magnifying glass helps Sybil make more careful observations with her eyes. The scissors allow her to cut into things to see what they look like on the inside. The test tube allows Sybil to see what happens when she mixes things.

If using actual magnifying glasses, give them to students now. Students may need an opportunity to observe some items using the magnifying glass. If actual magnifying glasses are not being used, give students a copy of Sybil's Magnifying Glass *memory trigger to make. The purpose of the magnifying glass is to remind students how scientists think.)*

Sybil works in a very exciting place — a laboratory. Sybil's laboratory is a very busy place with many experiments going on. Sybil is very curious and loves to make observations, to set up experiments, and to think scientifically.

That day, as Sybil was writing her observations for the morning in her science journal, Jordan the Judge stopped by. Jordan and Sybil were going to play in the softball game at the annual picnic.

"Hi, Jordan," said Sybil. "I will be ready as soon as I finish recording my observations."

Sybil locked the laboratory, and they left to enjoy the softball game and Crystal Pond Woods picnic.

Sybil and Jordan never finished the softball game. Sybil chased a long fly ball into the woods and, while looking for the ball, she discovered a group of creatures she had never seen before! Sybil was very excited, as scientists are when they make a new discovery. Sybil, with Jordan's help, gathered the new creatures together and took them back to her laboratory where she could make careful observations.

Sybil was the first scientist in Crystal Pond Woods to discover the creatures. After she safely returned to her laboratory with the creatures, Sybil began to think scientifically. First, she read her science books to see if any other scientists had written about these creatures, but she could find no information in her books.

Next, Sybil took out a brand-new science journal for her observations of the creatures. Sybil wanted to organize the new information about the creatures in order to classify them. **Classifying** is organizing into groups. Since no one had given her any rules to follow for creating her groups, Sybil had to make some observations of their characteristics, or **attributes,** in order to classify these creatures.

(Project the colorized set of Sybil's creatures and discuss the characteristics/attributes that Sybil might observe in them.)

Sybil only had four cages in which to put the creatures. She wanted to develop a way of organizing the creatures so that not only would they fit in her four cages but so all the creatures in each cage would be alike in some ways as well. Sybil, like all scientists, is very patient. She knows that it may take many tries before she is able to find a way or rule that works.

To get started, Sybil makes an educated guess which scientists call an **hypothesis**. Sybil wrote the hypothesis in her science journal. She tried to put the creatures in the cages according to how many feet they had.

(Label the cages 6 feet, 4 feet, 2 feet, and no feet. As you begin to put creatures into the cages, students will realize that some of the creatures have 1 or 3 feet. Since there is no place for these creatures, this hypothesis does not work.)

Sybil discovered that her hypothesis was not going to work. She did not have enough cages for all the different number of feet. What a unique group of creatures she had found!

(At this point, have the students offer other suggestions about how to group the creatures back into the cages. There is no one right answer for classifying the laboratory creatures. Once the class has discovered a way of putting the creatures in the

cages, finish reading the story. If no possible way is found, use the alternate ending.)

After successfully classifying all of the newly found creatures, Sybil sat down to record in her science journal her observations and her final rules for classifying the creatures. Since Sybil had tried many hypotheses before she found one that worked, she was very tired but very happy when she finally finished with her journal.

ALTERNATE ENDING

Sybil was not discouraged that she had not found a way that would work to sort and classify these creatures. She knew she could sleep on it that night and would certainly have a new idea for tomorrow.

Sybil's Magnifying Glass

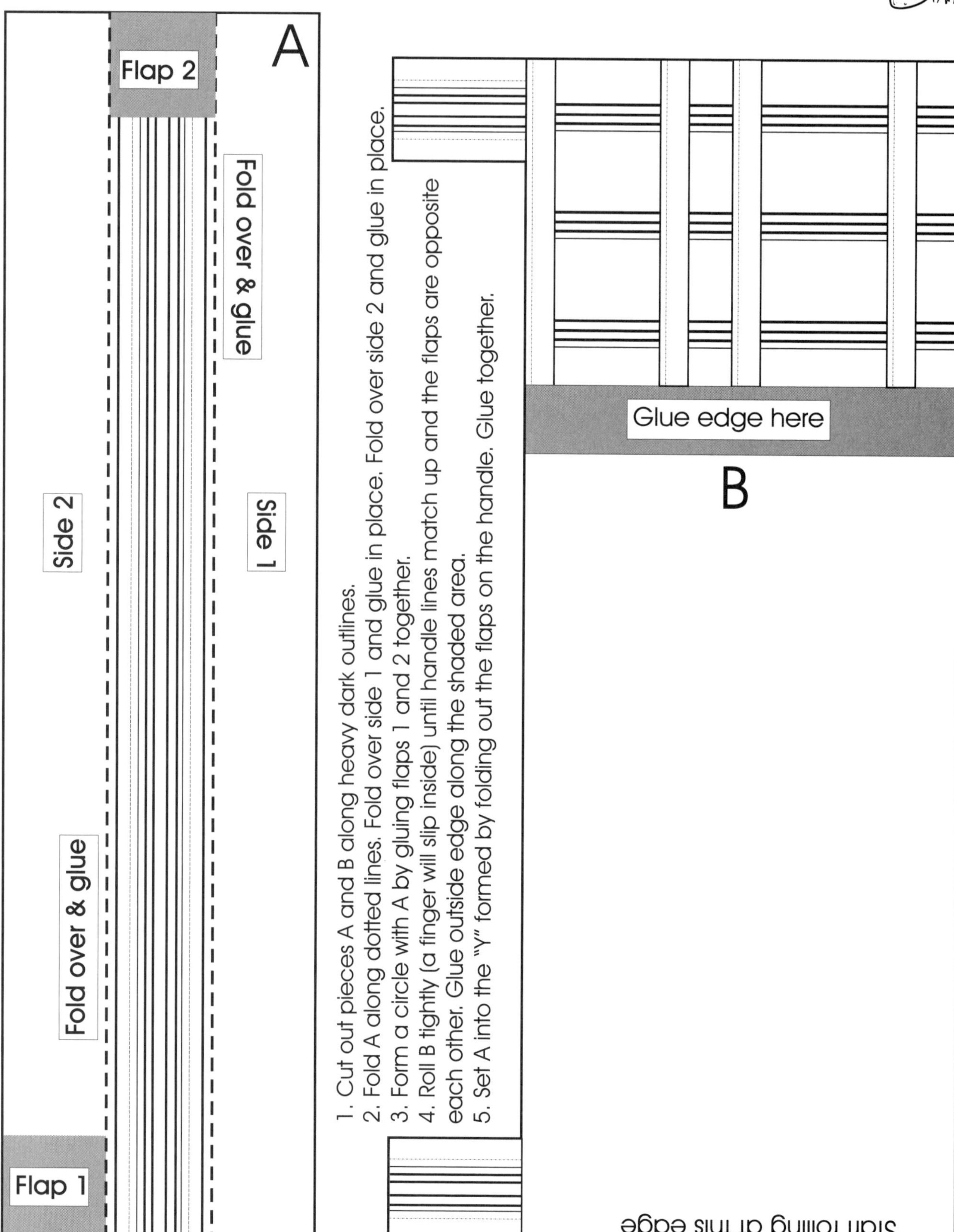

Sybil's Creatures

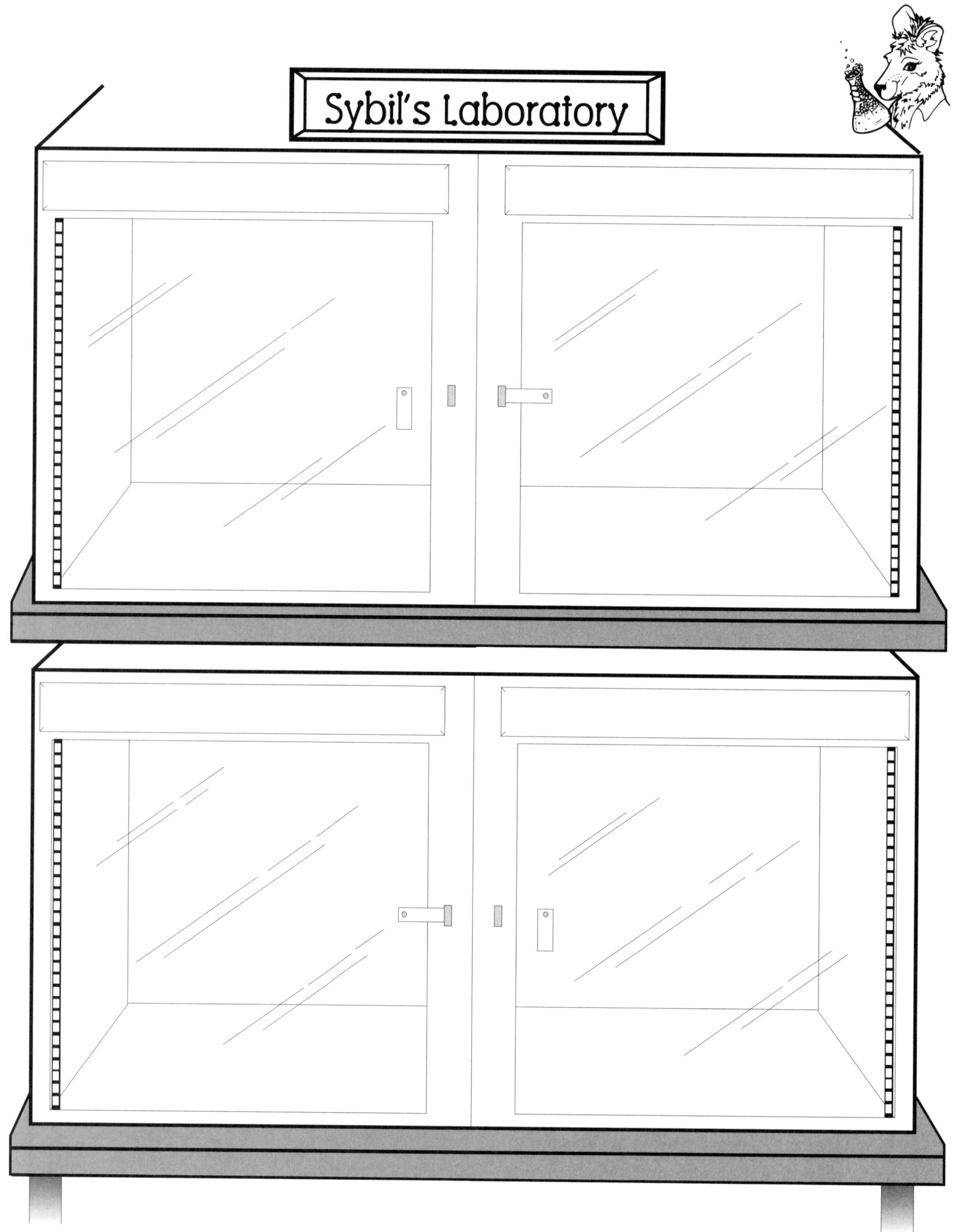
Sybil's Laboratory

Loose Laboratory Limpets

Help put these limpets back in their cages in Sybil's laboratory. Cut them out, group them, and glue them into their cages. Thanks!

Name ____________________

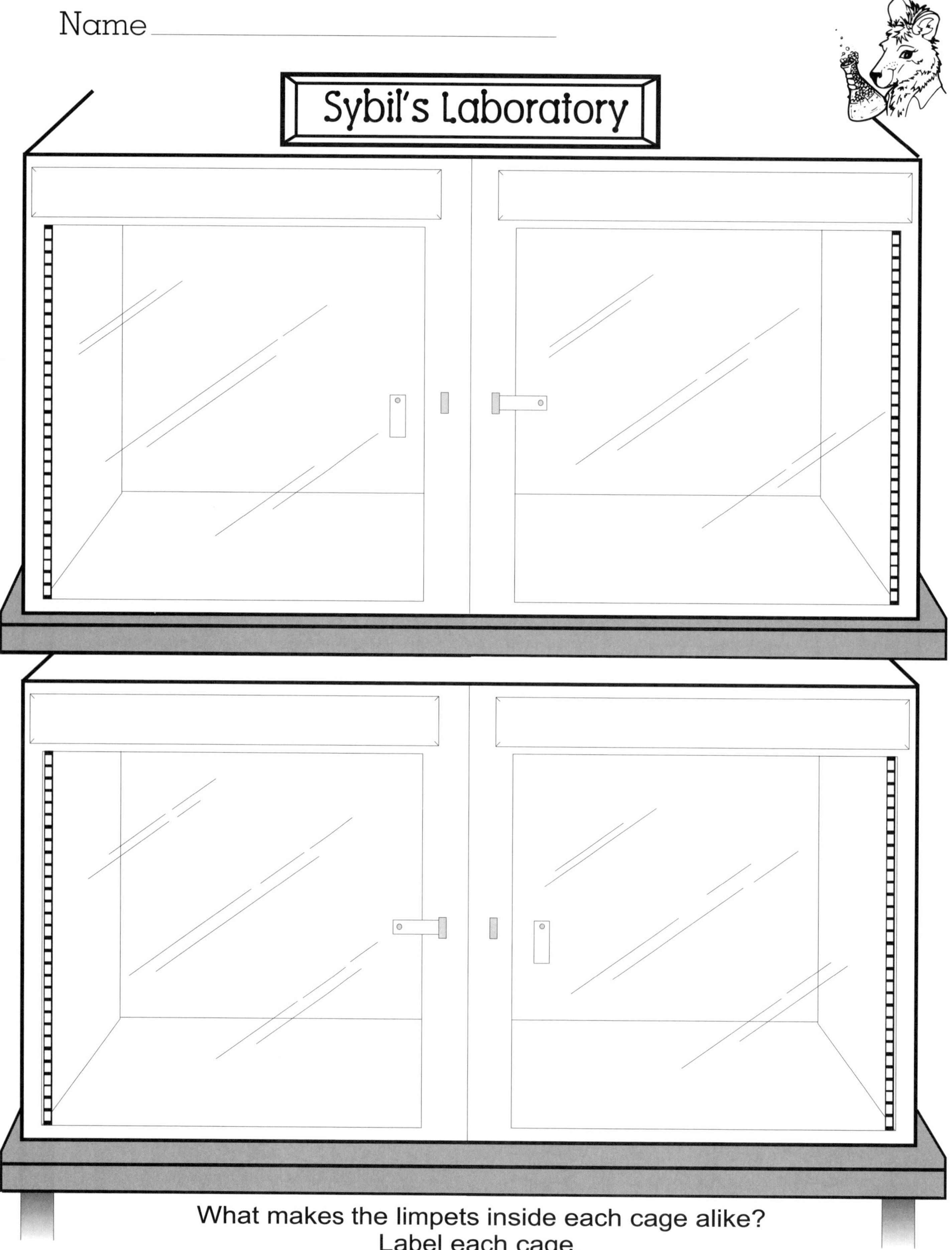

What makes the limpets inside each cage alike?
Label each cage.

SCIENTIST THINKING
WHOLE CLASS
LESSON 2

PURPOSE

In this lesson, students will be introduced to another type of **analytical thinking: compare and contrast.** The lesson is designed as a class discussion.

TEACHER MATERIALS

For duplication:

— PETS™ Behavioral Checklist – *Scientist Thinking*
— *Sybil's Scientific Pairs* cards
— class set of *Thinking about Alike and Different 1-2*
— class set of *Thinking about Alike and Different 3-4*

— OR a collection of items as pictured or described on *Sybil's Scientific Pairs* cards

STUDENT MATERIALS

— pencils

LESSON PLAN

1. Review with students these concepts introduced in Lesson 1. A scientist:
   — makes careful observations.
   — looks for common characteristics (or attributes).

2. This lesson involves looking at two things and trying to determine how they are alike and how they are different. Have students sit near the teacher, such as on the floor near the teacher's chair. Say to students:

Sybil enjoys thinking scientifically about the world around her. Often she will think about how two things are alike and different. Help Sybil decide how these pairs are alike and different.

Show students a pair of *Sybil's Scientific Pairs* cards (or the actual items pictured on a pair of cards). Ask students to suggest ways these two things (a button and a zipper, for example) are alike – what characteristics or attributes do they share? Spend some time with this; don't stop when the first lull in the thinking occurs. Students must get past the ordinary ideas that will come out first in order to capture the deeper, more creative similarities. After brainstorming comparisons for as long as possible, ask the students to contrast the two items by suggesting ways they are different. Follow this procedure for comparing and contrasting the other pairs suggested by the cards. Using actual items

when available may be more engaging for students, but for more abstract ideas, the cards themselves work best to stimulate brainstorming.

CHALLENGE PAGE

Thinking about Alike and Different 1-4

3. Distribute the challenge pages which are to be done independently in class. These pages may be tiered by giving *Alike and Different 1-2* to students who appear to need more direct structure and *Alike and Different 3-4* to students who are ready to think more open-endedly and create their own *Alike and Different* drawings to compare and contrast.

DIAGNOSTIC NOTES

Look for students who analytically compare and contrast. Also look for students who do so in a creative or unusual way.

A checklist for the whole class lesson is provided. The following is a short summary of student behaviors to note:

IDENTIFIES ATTRIBUTES – Look for students who understand the concept of attributes (or characteristics) and identify them accurately. They understand, for example, that similarly shaped shadows would be a common attribute of the shadow-producing objects.

CREATES CLASSIFICATION SYSTEMS – Look for students who create a viable, discrete classification system. This lesson does not offer as many opportunities to observe this characteristic as Whole Class Lesson 1 in this unit.

DEMONSTRATES UNIQUE STRATEGIES – Look for students who find unique or unusual ways in which two things are alike or different. They will often change course and try new approaches that other students have not considered.

DEFERS JUDGMENT – Look for students who wait before offering an answer, carefully weighing various options. These students may also think of ideas for pairs after the class has gone ahead.

DRAWS RELATIONSHIPS – Look for students who know or want to know specific facts about the world around them. Some students will bring a vast array of knowledge to class with them. This in itself does not indicate a talented student, but combining this with some of the other characteristics will give the teacher a more thorough picture of the student's potential.

RECOGNIZES FLAWED REASONING – Look for students who recognize when an apparent connection between two things does not really work and can explain why.

RETAINS INFORMATION – When reviewing ideas from earlier lessons, look for students who clearly recall the concepts and then effectively apply them to the current lesson's activities. While many children may grasp concepts "in the moment" of the instructional lesson, these students exhibit the significant ability to retain and apply new learning across time.

Thinking about Alike and Different

Look for students who:

- complete the *Alike and Different* pages independently.
- exhibit creativity in their analyses.
- clearly understand the difference between comparing and contrasting.

NOTES

Sybil's Scientific Pairs 1

a button	**a zipper**
a back pack	**a lunch box**

Sybil's Scientific Pairs 2

a rain forest

a circus

a postage stamp

a good book

Sybil's Scientific Pairs 3

a fairy tale

a song

the wind

a movie

Sybil's Scientific Pairs 4

a seashell

a tree

the door

friend-ship

Sybil's Scientific Pairs 5

a rainbow

a window

a pencil

a map

Name ______________________________

Thinking about Alike and Different 1

Alike		Different

Name ___________________________

Thinking about Alike and Different 2

Alike		Different

Name ____________________

Thinking about Alike and Different 3

Alike		Different

Name ______________________________

Thinking about Alike and Different 4

Alike		Different

SCIENTIST THINKING
SMALL GROUP
LESSON 1

PURPOSE

The purpose of this lesson is to allow capable students further experiences in **analytical thinking**. They will practice the observation and classification skills that a scientist uses.

TEACHER MATERIALS

For duplication

— *PETS™ Small Group Checklist* for each student

— a *Curiosity Caboodle* for each pair or triad of students. This can be a collection of rocks, shells, buttons, or other items for sorting

— optional magnifying glasses

LESSON PLAN

1. Give each pair or triad of students a collection of items for sorting. The idea is that the items will have many varied characteristics. Natural items such as rocks and shells work well, as do buttons or similar items. Each collection should have at least a dozen items for sorting.

2. Remind the students about Sybil's analytical thinking and how she examines items closely for detail in order to create groups or sets of items.

3. Tell each group of students to sort the items in their *Curiosity Caboodle* collection. Do not provide any more instructions; in fact, it is often helpful to walk a distance away and just let the students "dive in" to figure out for themselves how to begin.

4. When the students say they have sorted their entire *Caboodle*, check their work by asking them to tell you why the groups go together. Students need to be able to determine discrete groups that do not make it possible for an item to belong in more than one group. Point out errors by asking questions such as, "Where does this button go? It's pink and it has two holes. Should it go in your pink group or in your group with two holes?" Students should then continue until they can create at least two discrete groups from their *Caboodle* items.

5. When students have established an effecive discrete set of groups, sweep the *Curiosity Caboodle* items back together and ask the students to re-sort them again in a

different way. Grouping and re-grouping forces deeper analytical thinking and flexibility of thought.

DIAGNOSTIC NOTES

Look for students who:

- — determine discrete groups – groups that do not make it possible for an item to belong in more than one group at a time.
- — adapt when they realize their grouping will not work. Some students will stay with a bad choice, whereas others easily adjust to have successful groups.
- — rearrange the objects numerous ways.
- — use creative or unusual ways of sorting.

NOTES

SCIENTIST THINKING
SMALL GROUP
LESSON 2

PURPOSE

The purpose of this lesson is to provide students with the opportunity to examine various aspects of objects, pair them, and then find another pair that has the same relationship. This activity requires both creative and analytical thinking as students arrange the cards according to **analogies.**

TEACHER MATERIALS

For duplication:

— *PETS™ Small Group Checklist* for each student

— *Sybil's Picture Analogy Card Deck* for the group or one set for each pair of students. Prepare these ahead of time, copying them on colored paper (a different color for each deck) and laminating.

LESSON PLAN

1. Introduce students to the concept of *analogies* by providing some simple examples. The following are some possibilities:

hand is to glove as foot is to shoe
green is to grass as brown is to dirt

Ask students to brainstorm some of their own analogies to be sure they understand.

Activity 1:
2. This activity can be done in pairs or as a group. Give each working group a *Sybil's Picture Analogy Card Deck.* Have the students organize the deck into a series of accurate analogies. Each analogy will use four cards and all the cards should be used to make twelve different analogies.

3. *Sybil's Picture Analogy Card Deck* allows for a variety of matchings. Some matchings are more obvious than others. Similar, opposite, action of the objects, characteristics, whole to part, object to group, or mathematical relationships are some of the matchings possible in the cards. Show students the deck of cards but do not tell them the possible relationships. Remind students that the order is important. For example, if the analogy is:

"*cat* is to kitten as *dog* is to puppy"

it is important for the adult animals to be first on both sides.

4. Depending on the student's viewpoint, cards can be combined in a variety of ways. Some combinations may not be obvious, requiring an explanation from the student. Accept any analogy that offers a reasonable relationship. If no reasonable combination of cards can be found to complete the second part of the analogy, then the first part of the relationship and possibly other already completed analogies must be regrouped to make a larger number of correct analogies.

Activity 2:
5. Let each student in turn pick any four cards from *Sybil's Picture Analogy Card Deck* and create an analogy from them. As some combinations may not be obvious, require an explanation from the student. Accept any analogy that offers a reasonable relationship.

DIAGNOSTIC NOTES

Listening to the reasoning is just as important as keeping track of the number of reasonable combinations expressed in the correct format.

Look for students who:
- — put together valid analogies.
- — use the correct ***A:B :: C:D*** order.
- — change previous analogies in order to find a better fit.
- — construct creative and unusual analogies.

Sybil's Picture Analogy Card Deck

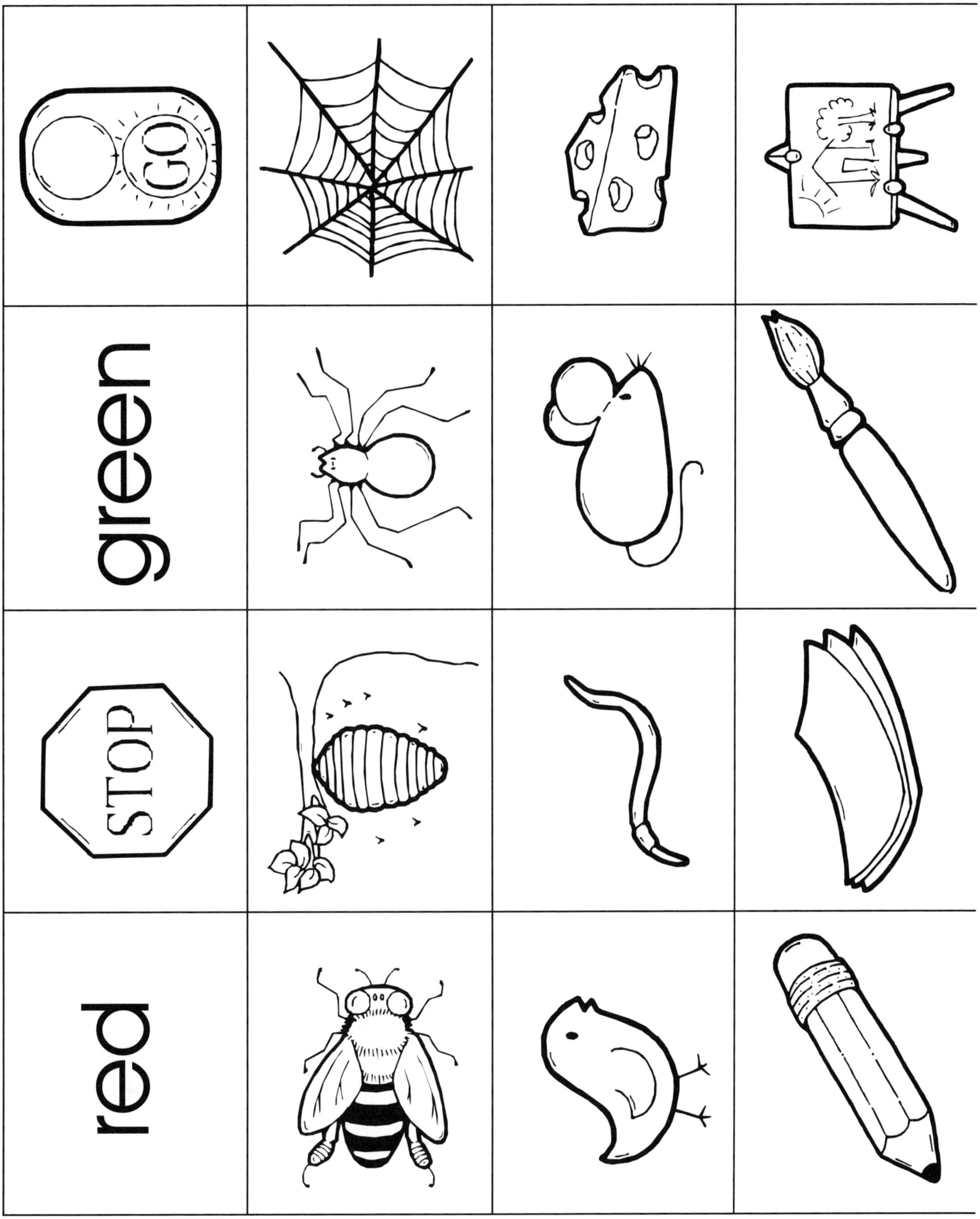

GO

green

STOP

red

Sybil's Picture Analogy Card Deck

Sybil's Picture Analogy Card Deck

pan	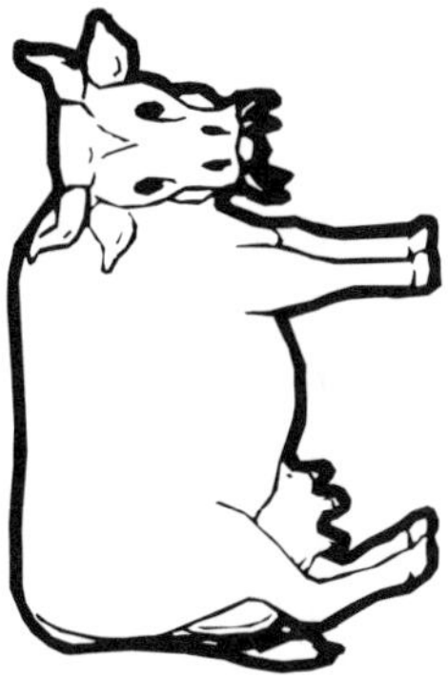	4	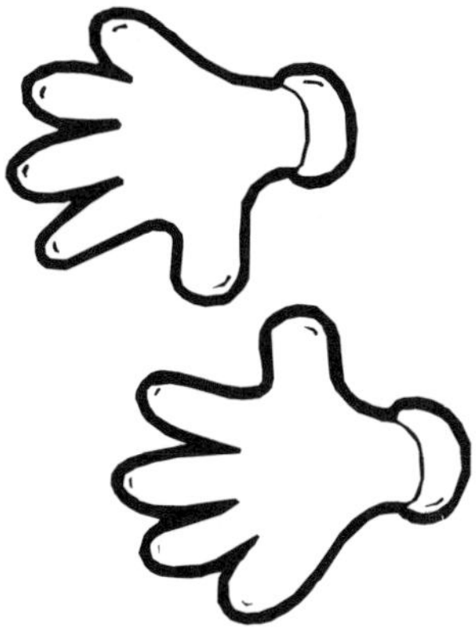
nap	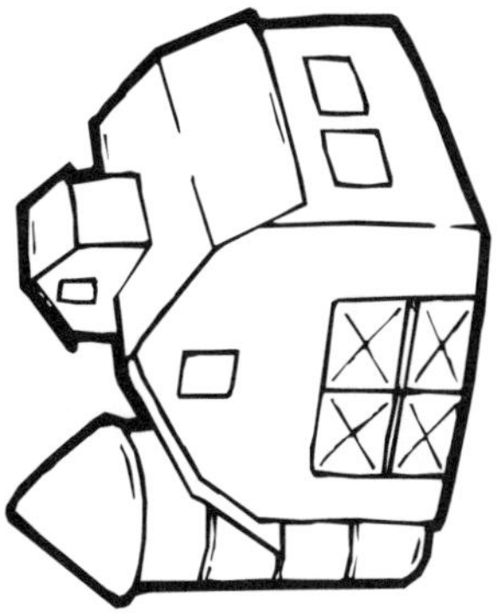	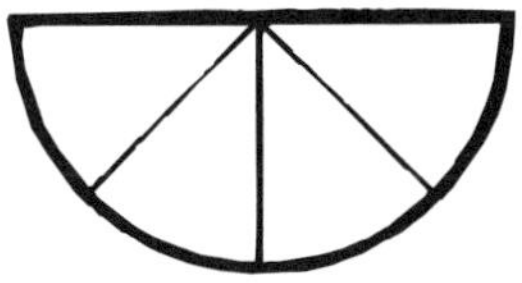	10
321		8	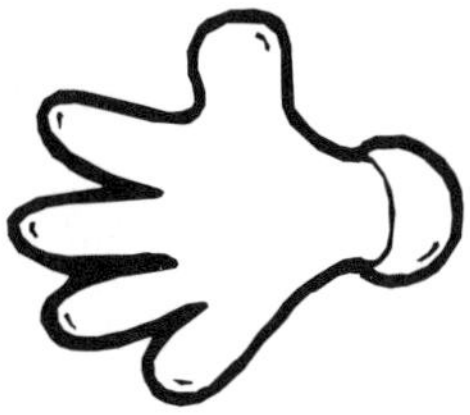
123		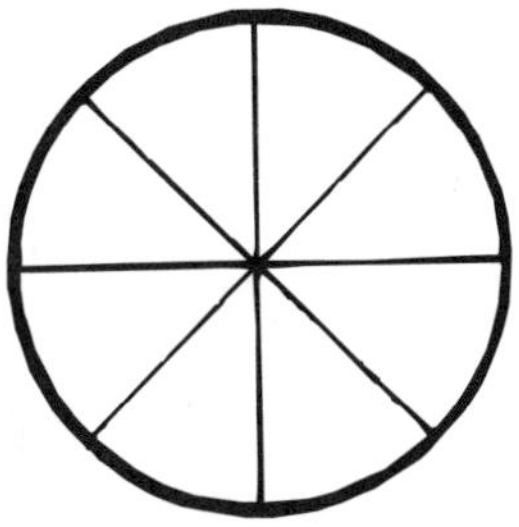	5

Ask me what I did in Thinking Skills today!
. . . looking for ways things are alike and ways to group them . . .
SYBIL

Ask me what I did in Thinking Skills today!
. . . looking for ways things are alike and ways to group them . . .
SYBIL

Ask me what I did in Thinking Skills today!
. . . looking for ways things are alike and ways to group them . . .
SYBIL

Ask me what I did in Thinking Skills today!
. . . looking for ways things are alike and ways to group them . . .
SYBIL

Yolanda

the

Yarnspinner

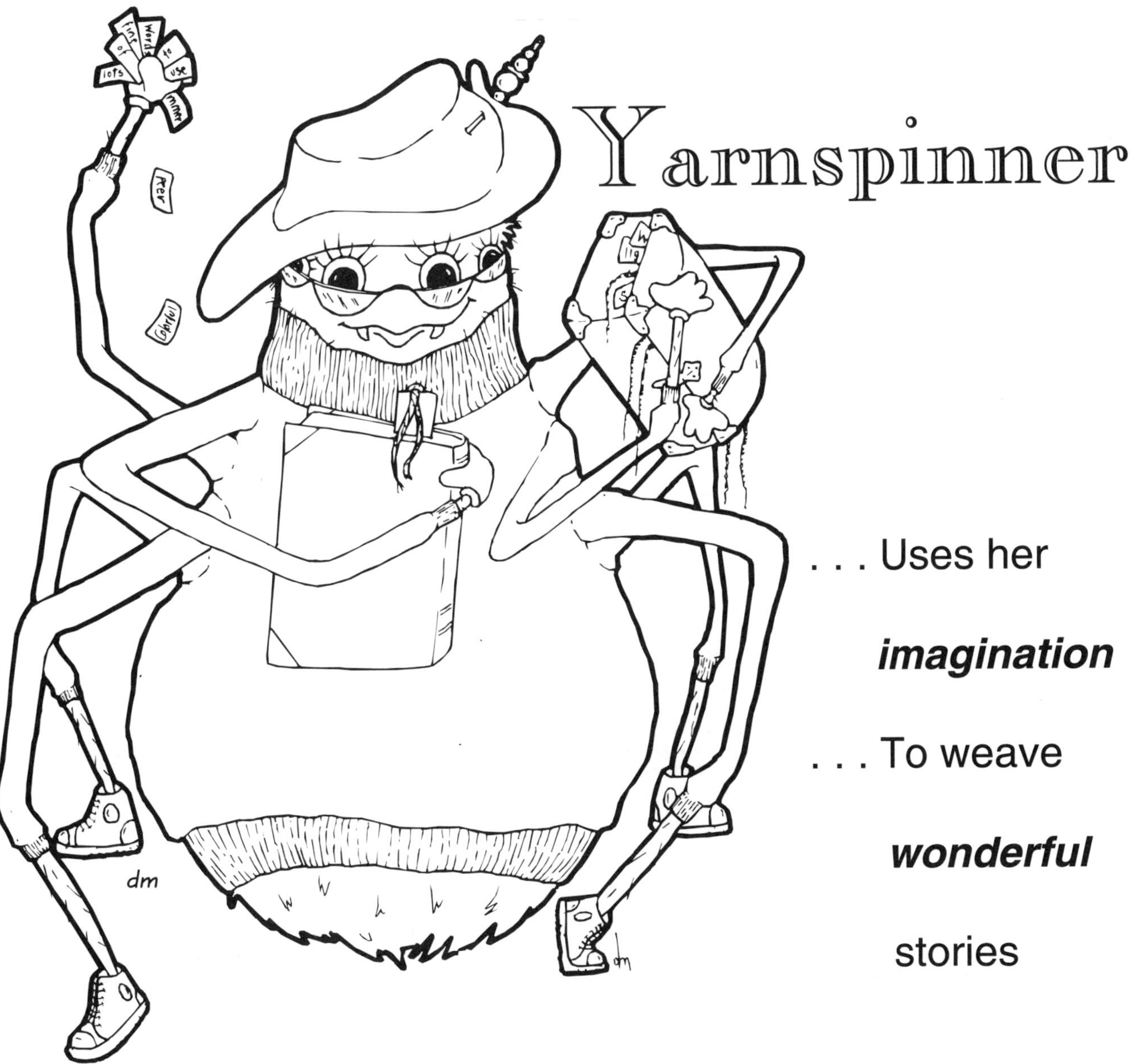

. . . Uses her

imagination

. . . To weave

wonderful

stories

Divergent/Creative Thinking

List names of students as each behavior appears. **Add checkmarks** after name if behavior is repeated. **Use a different color** of ink or pencil for each whole group lesson.	**PETS™** **Behavioral Checklist** **Yarnspinner Thinking** (creative/divergent thinking)	Teacher ______ Grade ______ Dates of whole group instruction: 1. ______ 2. ______

OFFERS MANY IDEAS (fluency)	**USES COLORFUL WORDS** TO ELICIT IMAGERY OR EMOTION (flexibility)
OFFERS UNIQUE OR UNCOMMON RESPONSES TO ELICIT IMAGERY OR EMOTION (originality)	**USES PHRASES** RATHER THAN SINGLE WORDS TO EXPRESS IDEAS (elaboration)
DISPLAYS UNUSUAL OR **MATURE SENSE OF HUMOR**	**USES ADVANCED VOCABULARY** IN A MATURE, ARTICULATE MANNER
RETAINS INFORMATION FROM PREVIOUS LESSONS	**PETS™ CLASSWORK** INDICATES AN OUTSTANDING ABILITY TO USE THIS THINKING SKILL

I see these behaviors in these students regularly during class time as well:	These students did not stand out during the PETS™ lessons, but I see these behaviors during regular class time:	Notes:

J

DIAGNOSTIC NOTES • YARNSPINNER THINKING

OFFERS MANY IDEAS (fluency) • *generates many ideas* • *all responses are acceptable* • *responses do not have to be creative*	**USES COLORFUL WORDS** TO ELICIT IMAGERY OR EMOTION (flexibility) • *uses colorful words* • *elicits visual images* • *elicits an emotional response*
OFFERS UNIQUE OR UNCOMMON RESPONSES TO ELICIT IMAGERY OR EMOTION (originality) • *shares uncommon or unique ideas* • *elicits visual images* • *elicits an emotional response*	**USES PHRASES** RATHER THAN SINGLE WORDS TO EXPRESS IDEAS (elaboration) • *uses descriptive phrases*
DISPLAYS UNUSUAL OR **MATURE SENSE OF HUMOR** • *understands your jokes* • *makes jokes you appreciate*	**USES ADVANCED VOCABULARY** IN A MATURE, ARTICULATE MANNER • *correctly uses words others do not know* • *expresses ideas in a more mature, articulate manner*
RETAINS INFORMATION FROM PREVIOUS LESSONS • *shares knowledge accurately during review* • *applies knowledge during activities*	**PETS™ CLASSWORK** INDICATES AN OUTSTANDING ABILITY TO USE THIS THINKING SKILL • *seatwork and/or challenge papers are exceptionally well done*

I see these behaviors in these students regularly during class time as well:	These students did not stand out during the PETS™ lessons, but I see these behaviors during regular class time:	Notes:
• *normally great creative thinkers*	• *normally great creative thinkers who "hid out" during the PETS™ lesson*	• *absentees* • *new students*

- *be generous — more inclusive than exclusive*
- *names can go in more than one box per answer*
- *be sure to add ✓s after names for multiple answers*
- *be sure to use different colors for each whole group lesson*

YARNSPINNER THINKING
WHOLE CLASS
LESSON 1

PURPOSE

The purpose of this lesson is to review and reinforce the concepts of **divergent creative thinking.** Students will learn about the art of storytelling from *Yolanda the Yarnspinner* who weaves colorful word pictures with her creative use of language. Students will learn that in divergent creative thinking:

— There are many possibilities.
— A creative imagination helps us see many possibilities in ordinary events, situations, and objects.
— Storytelling incorporates colorful words and phrasing.

TEACHER MATERIALS

For projection:

— *Yolanda the Yarnspinner* picture – a colorized Yolanda is available on the CD
— *Skeletal Sentences*

For duplication:

— *Yolanda the Yarns pinner* story to read aloud
— *PETS™ Behavioral Checklist – Yarnspinner Thinking*
— picture of Yolanda the Yarnspinner for each student to color
— class set of *Yolanda's Bookmarks*
— class set of *Super Sentences*
— class set of *Stupendous Statements*

— yarn

STUDENT MATERIALS

— crayons or colored pencils
— pencils
— glue
— scissors

LESSON PLAN

1. Introduce students to the lesson by asking if they have ever told a story. If so, they are *storytellers.* Ask students what characteristics make a good storyteller. Hopefully students will respond with *imagination, creativity,* and *interesting ideas.* Some story-tellers write their stories and others tell their stories. Ask students what some of their favorite stories are.

2. Explain to students that today they are going to meet *Yolanda the Yarnspinner* who uses her creative imagination to tell colorful stories. Project the picture of Yolanda. Students may color their pictures of Yolanda at this time or following the reading of Yolanda's story.

3. Read *Yolanda the Yarnspinner* story.

4. Review with the students these points from the story:
   — There are many possibilities in storytelling.
   — Good storytellers love to play with words and will use words in creative ways to make entertaining pictures in our minds.
   — Good storytellers enjoy searching for just the right word to make their word pictures vivid.

5. Give each student one of Yolanda's bookmarks and pieces of yarn to glue onto the bookmark. The bookmark is the memory trigger for this unit to help students remember to think like a storyteller during their activities.

6. To practice making sentences more colorful, use the words on Yolanda's list of *Skeletal Sentences* (subject-verb only). Project the cut-apart, individual words. Ask students to expand the sentences and make them "colorful" by answering the questions you ask about the sentences. Add their responses to the projected sentence in a variety of colored inks to illustrate the concept that you are using colorful words to make the sentences grow.

For example: Project the cut-apart words for the first sentence – "The boy ran"– so that they can be moved around as students add their colorful words. Ask the students questions such as these:
   — Is this a complete sentence? *(Yes, it is, because it has the requisite parts: a subject and a verb. However, we can make this sentence more colorful by thinking like Yolanda.)*
   — What kind of boy was he? *(Accept any reasonable response, and use a colored marker to insert the response between* "The" *and* "boy.")
   — Where did he run? *(Again, accept any reasonable response, and use another colored marker to insert the response in the appropriate spot.)*
   — How was he running? *(Accept reasonable adverbs and place in the appropriate place in the sentence with a different colored marker.)*
   — Why was he running there? *(This phrase will most likely end the sentence, but you may continue questioning in this manner until you have a sentence you think is colorful, sensible, and complete.)*

Have the students notice all the colors they were able to add to this sentence. You may use all the sentences provided, use just a few, or create your own.

CHALLENGE PAGES

Super Sentences *Stupendous Statements*

7. Distribute the challenge pages which are to be done independently in class. Tell students to sort the words that Yolanda has collected first – either as words to be treasured or recycled for later use. Then tell them to create vivid, colorful sentences using words they put in the treasure chest plus any other interesting words they need. Both the word choices students make and the types of sentences they write are important aspects of the challenge pages.

DIAGNOSTIC NOTES

A checklist of student behaviors to note during the whole class lesson is provided. These behaviors are very similar to those listed in the unit about Isabel the Inventor as both units involve divergent thinking.

OFFERS MANY IDEAS (fluency) – All responses are acceptable. Look for students who generate many ideas.

USES COLORFUL WORDS (flexibility) – The ability to generate a varied vocabulary that creates vivid visual images or elicits emotional responses reflects a student's flexibility of thought.

OFFERS UNIQUE OR UNCOMMON RESPONSES (originality) – Record the students who propose unusual responses that elicit visual images or emotional reactions.

USES PHRASES (elaboration) – Look for students who use phrases rather than single words. This shows the ability to elaborate with words.

DISPLAYS UNUSUAL OR MATURE SENSE OF HUMOR – This unit offers many opportunities for students to incorporate humor. Look for those students with a subtle or advanced sense of humor.

USES ADVANCED VOCABULARY – Look for students who correctly use a large vocabulary. Also look for students who express themselves in a mature, articulate manner.

RETAINS INFORMATION – When reviewing ideas from earlier lessons, look for students who clearly recall the concepts and then effectively apply them to the current lesson's activities. While many children may grasp concepts "in the moment" of the instructional lesson, these students exhibit the significant ability to retain and apply new learning across time.

Super Sentences
Stupendous Statements
Look for students who:
- — determine vivid words and place them in the treasure chest.
- — use their vivid words, in combination with original words, to create interesting and colorful sentences.
- — display an advanced sense of humor in their sentence development.

YOLANDA THE YARNSPINNER

On a bright, sunny day in Crystal Pond Woods, Yolanda the Yarnspinner was in her tree doing her second favorite thing, spinning a beautiful web. As she was spinning away, that mischievous raccoon, Rascal Raccoon, came running up.

"Yolanda, Yolanda!" he yelled. "Please, help me. I need your help."

Yolanda stopped spinning her web and looked down at Rascal Raccoon. She could not imagine why he would need her help, but she was polite enough not to say so.

"Of course I will help you," said Yolanda, "if I can."

"The most exciting thing has happened to me, and I want to share it at the community campfire tonight," said Rascal Raccoon. "I am afraid that once I start telling the story, I will get nervous, and it will not sound nearly as exciting. Please, Yolanda, please help me with my story. Everyone in Crystal Pond Woods knows that you are the best at spinning yarns."

Rascal Raccoon was correct. Yolanda is known far and wide as one of the best yarnspinners. It is her favorite thing to do. **Spinning yarns** is another way of saying she is a storyteller. The creatures of Crystal Pond Woods love to listen to Yolanda spin her stories. One reason Yolanda is very good at telling stories is that she has a very creative imagination. She can turn everyday activities or objects into an entertaining web of magic. Sometimes her stories are make-believe, and sometimes they are real, but they are always entertaining.

Another reason Yolanda is so good at spinning yarns is that she knows a lot of words. She always searches for just the right word to put magic into her story. In her trunk of yarns, Yolanda

has all kinds of words. She has words that rhyme, words that imitate sounds, and words that begin with the same sound. She uses words to paint pictures that you can see clearly in your mind. Yolanda is an artist with words.

Rascal Raccoon had certainly picked the right friend for help!

Yolanda reached into her trunk and drew out some yarn. She finds it very helpful to her creative process if she winds yarn while she thinks of her story. Sometimes Yolanda spins her yarn to make a bookmark. Even though Yolanda is a storyteller, she loves to read other people's stories and can always use a good bookmark. After choosing the yarn, Yolanda began to make her bookmark. She offered yarn to Rascal Raccoon so he could make a bookmark. Now Yolanda was ready to help Rascal Raccoon.

"First," she said, "tell me about the exciting thing that happened to you."

"Well," started Rascal Raccoon, "early this morning I went through Dudley the Detective's yard, saw his open window, and climbed in through the window. There I saw Rosalyn Robin take Dudley's badge! Then I climbed out the window, ran through the backyard, and climbed over the fence."

"You are right, Rascal Raccoon," Yolanda replied. "You saw something very exciting, but you are not using exciting words to describe what happened to you. I will help you spin a more colorful story. First, what kind of morning was it?"

"It was a bright, sunny morning," answered Rascal Raccoon.

"Bright and sunny are colorful words. Be sure that you include those words when you tell your story," said Yolanda. "What did Dudley's yard look like?"

"His yard was very shiny because of the dew on the ground," replied Rascal Raccoon.

Yolanda knew the perfect word for Rascal Raccoon to use to describe the yard. "The yard **sparkled** in the sunlight," she suggested.

Rascal Raccoon was very impressed. Yolanda was very good with words.

"What made you look at Dudley's window?" continued Yolanda.

"Well," said Rascal Raccoon, "the curtains were flying out of the window blowing in the wind."

"Hmmm," murmured Yolanda as she wound yarn around her pencil. "The curtains were **billowing** in the wind."

"Wow, Yolanda," cried Rascal Raccoon. "It was a bright, sunny morning. The yard **sparkled** in the sunlight. Dudley the Detective's curtains were **billowing** in the wind. Rosalyn Robin's wings **swished** as she flew in the window. I thought of "swish" because that is how the wings sounded as she flew."

"You are doing great!" exclaimed Yolanda. "You are very creative. What happened after Rosalyn Robin flew in the window?"

"I climbed in the window and saw her take Dudley the Detective's badge. Then she flew to her nest in the apple tree," continued Rascal Raccoon.

"I know we can think of a few colorful words to use," said Yolanda as she spun her yarn. "Why don't you use **peered** instead of looked. What did Dudley's badge look like?"

"Well, it was **shiny** and **gold**. I think I'm beginning to get the idea, Yolanda. When I tell my story, I should try to use words that will paint a picture of what I saw," said Rascal Raccoon.

"You are going to be a great storyteller at the community campfire tonight. I can't wait to hear your entire story," replied Yolanda.

"Yolanda, I need to go practice my story. Is it okay if I keep the yarn bookmark to remind me of all the different kinds of words I can use in my story?" asked Rascal Raccoon.

"Yes," said Yolanda, "Tonight I will be cheering you on as you tell your exciting story. Good luck!" Yolanda waved good-bye to Rascal Raccoon with four of her eight legs.

Yolanda's Bookmarks

Cut out the bookmarks. Decorate Yolanda's sweater with pieces of yarn glued in place. Be sure to allow 8 pieces to dangle from the bottom — Yolanda's legs, of course!

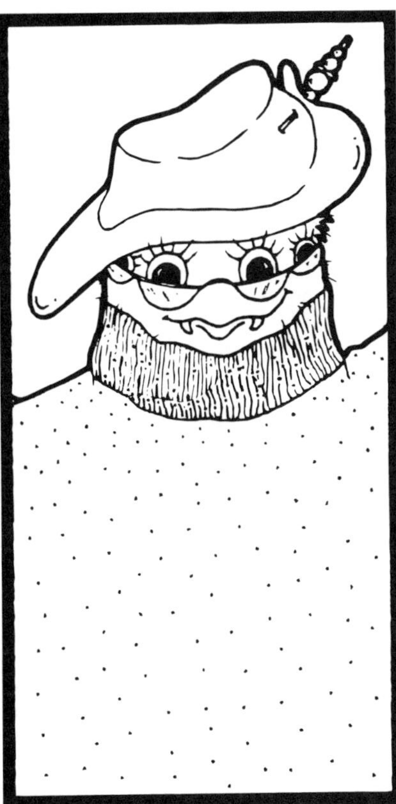

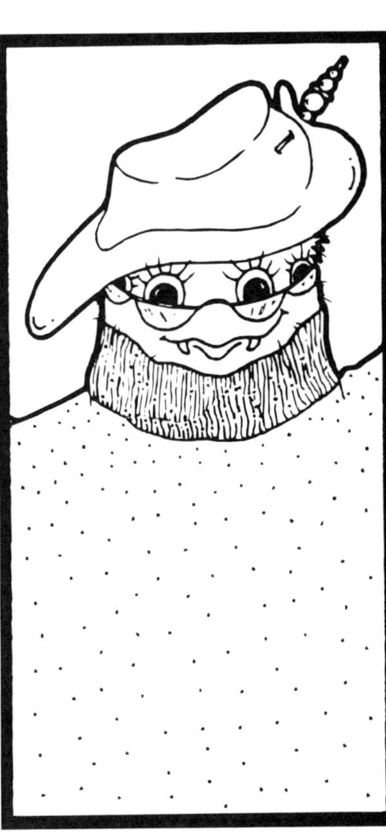

Skeletal Sentences

The boy ran

My mother reads

The dog barked

Our house sits

The baby is crying

Name: ______________________________

Super Sentences!

Separate these words that Yolanda has collected into two groups. "Treasure" the vivid, colorful words and recycle the others! Draw a line from each word to one of the containers.

Now use some of those "treasured" words to create colorful, lively sentences that will make Yolanda proud! Add any other interesting words you need.

____

____

____

____

____

____

____

Name: ____

Stupendous Statements!

Separate these words that Yolanda has collected into two groups. "Treasure" the vivid, colorful words and recycle the others! Draw a line from each word to one of the containers.

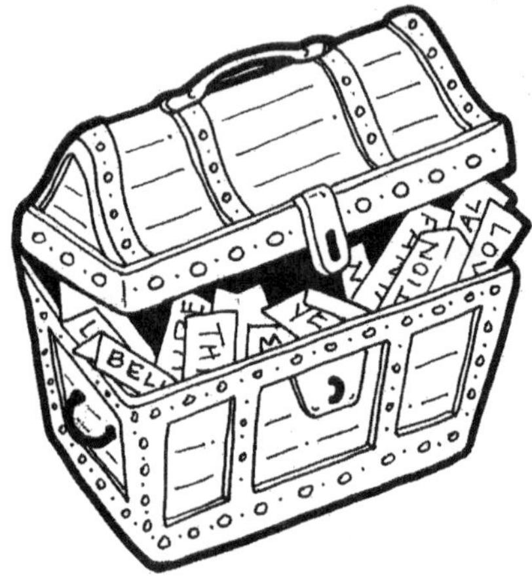

apple **bark** **chop**

kitten **coming** **said**

halt **several** **fantastic**

large **blaze** **brilliant**

jolly **high** **delicious**

tart

demand

answer **gigantic** **whoosh**

walks **hilarious** **skips**

Now use some of those "treasured" words to create colorful, lively sentences that will make Yolanda proud! Add any other interesting words you need.

____

____

____

____

____

____

____

YARNSPINNER THINKING
WHOLE CLASS
LESSON 2

PURPOSE

The purpose of this lesson is to review and reinforce the concepts of creative thinking in the **storytelling** process by incorporating colorful words and phrases into student writing. Students will create stories using colorful language to create visual images and elicit emotional responses. Students will review these concepts of divergent creative thinking:

— In creative thinking, there are many possibilities.
— A creative imagination is a useful tool for a storyteller.
— Storytelling incorporates colorful words and phrasing.

TEACHER MATERIALS

For projection:

— *Good News! Bad News!*

For duplication:

— *PETS™ Behavioral Checklist – Yarnspinner Thinking*
— class set of *What Good News! What Bad News!*
— optional set of *Making News* for capable writers

— one copy of either ***Fortunately*** by Remy Charlip or ***That's Good*** by Margery Cuyler

STUDENT MATERIALS

— crayons or colored pencils
— pencils

LESSON PLAN

1. Review with students the concepts of divergent thinking related to creative *story-telling*. A creative imagination sees many possibilities in ordinary events, situations, and objects, and a creative storyteller uses colorful language to relate what happens effectively.

2. Read aloud to the students ***Fortunately*** by Remy Charlip or ***That's Good! That's Bad!*** by Margery Cuyler. Ask students to describe any pattern they see in the story, either in the words or in the illustrations. Ask them also to identify any words or phrases which they find particularly colorful.

3. Following the reading of one of the books, project and read the sample *Good News! Bad News!* Have students identify and discuss the pattern that the story follows.

CHALLENGE PAGES

What Good News! What Bad News!
Making News

4. Ask students to use their creative thinking to write their own original stories which follow the *Good News/Bad News* pattern on the blank *What Good News! What Bad News!* challenge page. Remind them to make good use of colorful words and phrases whenever possible. Capable students might do the more difficult challenge pages, *Making News,* instead or as an additional follow-up. In *Making News,* students must plan ahead to incorporate an unusual prompt into the middle of a *Good News/Bad News* type of story. Developing a smooth flow throughout presents the students with an exceptional challenge.

DIAGNOSTIC NOTES

A checklist of student behaviors to note during the whole class lesson is provided. These behaviors are very similar to those listed in the unit about Isabel the Inventor as both units involve divergent thinking.

OFFERS MANY IDEAS (fluency) – All responses are acceptable. Look for students who generate many ideas.

USES COLORFUL WORDS (flexibility) – Look for students who use varied colorful words to create visual images or elicit emotional reactions.

OFFERS UNIQUE OR UNCOMMON RESPONSES (originality) – Record the students who propose unusual original responses that elicit visual images or emotional reactions.

USES PHRASES (elaboration) – Look for students who use phrases rather than single words. This shows the ability to elaborate with words.

DISPLAYS UNUSUAL OR MATURE SENSE OF HUMOR – This unit offers many opportunities for students to incorporate humor. Look for those students who display a subtle or advanced sense of humor.

USES ADVANCED VOCABULARY – Look for students who correctly use a large vocabulary. Also look for students who express themselves in a mature, articulate manner.

RETAINS INFORMATION – When reviewing ideas from earlier lessons, look for students who clearly recall the concepts and then effectively apply them to the current lesson's activities. While many children may grasp concepts "in the moment" of the instructional lesson, these students exhibit the significant ability to retain and apply new learning across time.

What Good News! What Bad News! and ***Making News***

Look for students who:

— use of colorful words and advanced vocabulary.
— follow the established good news/bad news story pattern.
— develop a smooth flow throughout their stories.
— write stories which display an unusual or advanced sense of humor.

NOTES

Good News! Bad News!

1. Good news!

   Mary has a new storybook.

2. Bad news!

   Some pages are missing!

3. Good news!

   Yolanda knows this story.

4. Bad news!

   Yolanda forgot the ending!

5. Good news!

   Mary can read the ending in the book. Those pages are there!

Name ______________________________

What Good News! What Bad News!

1. Good news!

2. Bad news!

3. Good news!

4. Bad news!

5. Good news!

Name ________________________

Making News

Write the missing lines and draw pictures for this news story.

WHAT GOOD NEWS!

My cousin is coming over to play.

WHAT BAD NEWS!

____

Name ______________________________

WHAT GOOD NEWS!

There is ice cream in the freezer.

WHAT BAD NEWS!

____

Name ______________________________

WHAT GOOD NEWS!

____

AND, WHAT GOOD NEWS!

____

YARNSPINNER THINKING
SMALL GROUP
LESSON 1

PURPOSE

The purpose of this lesson is to give students the opportunity to display their creative thinking with **word play**. As demonstrated in the Torrance Test of Creativity, creative thinkers display fluency, flexibility, originality, and elaboration in their thinking. In addition, many researchers feel that another identifier of gifted students is an advanced sense of humor. This lesson provides students with an outlet for all these traits.

TEACHER MATERIALS

For duplication:
- — *PETS™ Small Group Checklist* for each student
- — *Radical Riddles* for each student

OR

- — chart paper for recording students' final riddles

STUDENT MATERIALS

- — pencils (if using worksheet)

LESSON PLAN

1. Students are going to write *riddles* about animals. Have them think of an animal, such as a pig. Next they list all the one-syllable words that go with this animal. Some examples might be *slop, ham, snout, boar, sow,* etc. Then they drop the first sound of this word. *Slop* would become *op*, *ham* becomes *am*, and so on.

The next step is to think of long words that begin with "op" or "am" or whatever. Then add the dropped sound to the beginning of the long word. A riddle then might be something like this: What do pigs do on their night out? Go to the "slop-era!" Or: How do injured pigs get to the hospital? In a "ham-bulance!"

2. The brainstorming for this activity should be done as a group with children helping one another for the best list of riddles. A variety of animals can be used.

3. Try to find a real audience for the riddles. Have students illustrate their riddles. These riddles often make an interesting bulletin board or can be part of the school newsletter or other published format.

DIAGNOSTIC NOTES

Look for students who:

- — understand and perform the wordplay.
- — enjoy the wordplay.
- — generate lots of ideas.
- — propose unique word combinations.
- — display an advanced sense of humor.

NOTES

STUDENT RIDDLES

1. What do cows do in math class?
2. What do you call horses who wear masks and play baseball?
3. What do dogs go on when there is a flood?
4. What happens when a rabbit dials zero?
5. What do you call rabbits from outer space?
6. What do rabbit doctors perform?
7. Who makes the rules when rabbits play baseball?
8. What do you call a cow with a hard shell on its back?
9. What do pigs plug their TVs into?
10. What do cows wear in the battle?
11. What is a cat's favorite dessert?
12. Why do cows curl up and roll away?
13. Why do pigs go to the North Pole?
14. What do you call a doghouse designer?
15. How can you tell black bunnies from white bunnies?
16. When does cat's fur fall off?

Written by 1st graders at Husmann Elementary School, Crystal Lake, Illinois

1. Cud-dition facts
2. Jump-ires!
3. Noah's Bark
4. He gets the hop-Erato!
5. Cotton Tailing!
6. Hop-enactions!
7. Major league jump-ires!
8. A farm-Adela!
9. Squeal-ectric outlets!
10. Suits of farm-our!
11. Mice cream!
12. Because they're pretending to be farm-adilloes!
13. To live in pig-loos!
14. A bark-itecht!
15. Because they're hop-isites!
16 Every claw-tumn!

Name ______________________

Radical Riddles

1. Think of an animal:

2. Brainstorm a list of one-syllable words that go with this animal:

4. Think of a long word that begins with what is left of each one-syllable word:

5. Add back the first sound of the one-syllable word to the long word:

3. Then cross out the beginning sound of each these words. Use a slash mark (/).

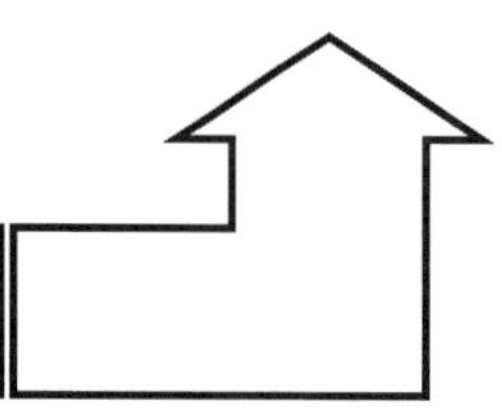

6. Use 2 of the new long words above in #5 as answers for your riddles:

7. Now write some riddles about your animal:

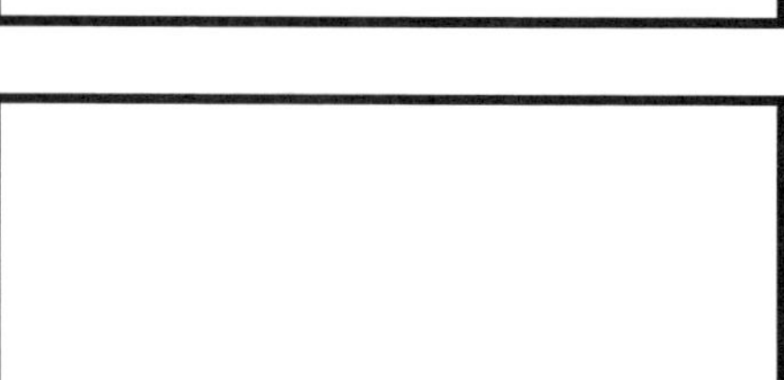

YARNSPINNER THINKING
SMALL GROUP
LESSON 2

PURPOSE

The purpose of this lesson is to review and reinforce the concepts of creative thinking in the *storytelling* process by incorporating colorful words and phrases into student writing. Students will create poems using colorful onomatopoeia to create visual images and elicit emotional responses. Students will review these concepts of divergent creative thinking:

— In creative thinking, there are many possibilities.
— A creative imagination is a useful tool for a storyteller.
— Storytelling incorporates colorful words and phrasing.

TEACHER MATERIALS

For duplication:
— *PETS™ Small Group Checklist* for each student

— chart paper

STUDENT MATERIALS

— crayons or colored pencils

LESSON PLAN

1. Students will learn how to create *onomatopoeia* poems. Onomatopoetic words imitate the sound they describe. Examples include *boom, crunch,* and *drip.*

2. Students are going to use their sound words to write poems which describe a special place. The examples on the following page can be read to students.

OUR BAND

In the band you hear a drum
BOOM! BOOM! BOOM!
Behind it is a little bell
RING-DING-DING
The cymbals make a clanging sound
CRASH! CRASH! CRASH!
The flutes can be heard all 'round
TWITTER, TWITTER, TWEET

The music's beat makes my feet go
TAP, TAP, TAP

And when it's done,
It's been such fun.
CLAP! CLAP! CLAP!

Written by 1st graders at Husmann Elementary School, Crystal Lake, Illinois

NOISES AT THE ZOO

The noises at the zoo
They sound kind of like this.
"Roar," roared the great big lion.
"Eeek, eeek," giggled the furry monkeys.
"Hee, hee, haw, haw," laughed the hyenas.
"Growl," growled the grizzly bear.
"Hiss," hissed the king cobra.
"Screech," scratched the bob cat.
"Snap," snapped the jaws of the alligator.
"Squeak," squeaked the gray mouse.
"Boom, boom, boom," went the elephant.
"Hush," said the zookeeper.

Written by first graders at Coventry Elementary School, Crystal Lake, Illinois

As the students were writing this poem, they tried to include colorful words as discussed in the Whole Class Lesson 1.

3. Have students brainstorm a list of words that sound like noises. The following are possible words to be used in the poems and added to the list brainstormed by students.

YOLANDA'S WORD BANK

WORDS THAT SOUND LIKE NOISES - onomatopoeia

buzz	crash	sizzle	clink	squeak
slam	clank	rat-a-tat	bang	purr
hush	splash	chirp	tinkle	thump
clap	hiss	slosh	pop	clang
swoosh	jingle	roar	eeek	jangle

WORDS TO USE INSTEAD OF "SAID"

roar	sang	tweeter	screech	hoot
howl	giggle	rumble	cry	stomp
yip	purr	laugh	growl	scratch
grumble	squawk	squeal	chirp	bark
croak	titter	smack	chuckle	chortle
loud	quiet	soft	whisper	shout
blare	hiss	yell	stomp	thunder

4. Have students imagine a very noisy place (the school band room, a big city, a zoo, etc.). As a group, write a poem using onomatopoeia that describes this special place. As students dictate the poem in a group, record their dictation, perhaps on a large poster which could be illustrated and displayed or published. Students can follow any poetic form that brings the sounds of their "place" to life. The first line of the poem should help to establish the location of the poem, and subsequent lines should be used to help the reader "hear" the sounds of their noisy place.

DIAGNOSTIC NOTES

Look for students who:

- — grasp the concept of onomatopoeia.
- — list lots of onomatopoeia.
- — use other colorful words or phrasing.
- — have an advanced vocabulary.
- — reflect a poetic bent.
- — display an advanced sense of humor.

NOTES

Ask me what I did
in
Thinking Skills
today!
. . . using my
imagination to
weave wonderful
yarns . . .

Ask me what I did
in
Thinking Skills
today!
. . . using my
imagination to
weave wonderful
yarns . . .

Ask me what I did
in
Thinking Skills
today!
. . . using my
imagination to
weave wonderful
yarns . . .

Ask me what I did
in
Thinking Skills
today!
. . . using my
imagination to
weave wonderful
yarns . . .

Max the Magician

... Looks for **_patterns_**

... To find **_a reasonable solution_**

Visual/Spatial Perception

PETS™

Behavioral Checklist

Magician Thinking

(visual/spatial perception)

List names of students as each behavior appears.

Add checkmarks after name if behavior is repeated.

Use a different color of ink or pencil for each whole group lesson.

Teacher ________________
Grade ______

Dates of whole group instruction: 1. ________ 2. ________

GRASPS CONCEPTS QUICKLY	**SEES INTERRELATIONSHIP OF CLUES;** COMBINES VISUAL CLUES TO SOLVE THE PROBLEM
COMMENTS INDICATE AN ABILITY TO **MANIPULATE SHAPES MENTALLY**	**DEFERS JUDGMENT;** GATHERS AND WEIGHS ALL INFORMATION BEFORE DECIDING ON A SOLUTION
SEES ANSWERS INTUITIVELY WITHOUT INTERMEDIATE STEPS	**IS TENACIOUS** IN APPROACH; WORKS DILIGENTLY TO THE END
RETAINS INFORMATION FROM PREVIOUS LESSONS	**PETS™ CLASSWORK** INDICATES AN OUTSTANDING ABILITY TO USE THIS THINKING SKILL

I see these behaviors in these students regularly during class time as well:	These students did not stand out during the PETS™ lessons, but I see these behaviors during regular class time:	Notes:

DIAGNOSTIC NOTES • MAGICIAN THINKING

<table>
<tr><td>GRASPS CONCEPTS QUICKLY
♦ sees perceptions presented quickly
♦ applies understanding to other situations quickly
♦ first to figure out correct answers</td><td>SEES INTERRELATIONSHIP OF CLUES; COMBINES VISUAL CLUES TO SOLVE THE PROBLEM
♦ combines information from various visual clues to establish the pattern</td></tr>
<tr><td>COMMENTS INDICATE AN ABILITY TO MANIPULATE SHAPES MENTALLY
♦ "sees" the shapes and/or the solution without needing to draw them on paper</td><td>DEFERS JUDGMENT; GATHERS AND WEIGHS ALL INFORMATION BEFORE DECIDING ON A SOLUTION
♦ waits until enough information is gathered to figure out the correct answer
♦ avoids guessing impulsively</td></tr>
<tr><td>SEES ANSWERS INTUITIVELY WITHOUT INTERMEDIATE STEPS
♦ arrives at correct answer without seeming to use intermediate steps
♦ not an impulsive guesser</td><td>IS TENACIOUS IN APPROACH; WORKS DILIGENTLY TO THE END
♦ works diligently to conclusion
♦ will NOT give up</td></tr>
<tr><td>RETAINS INFORMATION FROM PREVIOUS LESSONS
♦ shares knowledge accurately during review
♦ applies knowledge during activities</td><td>PETS™ CLASSWORK INDICATES AN OUTSTANDING ABILITY TO USE THIS THINKING SKILL
♦ seatwork and/or challenge papers are exceptionally well done</td></tr>
</table>

<table>
<tr><td>I see these behaviors in these students regularly during class time as well:
♦ normally great visual thinkers</td><td>These students did not stand out during the PETS™ lessons, but I see these behaviors during regular class time:
♦ normally great visual thinkers who "hid out" during the PETS™ lesson</td><td>Notes:
♦ absentees
♦ new students</td></tr>
</table>

- *be generous — more inclusive than exclusive*
- *names can go in more than one box per answer*
- *be sure to add ✓s after names for multiple answers*
- *be sure to use different colors for each whole group lesson*

MAGICIAN THINKING
WHOLE CLASS
LESSON 1

PURPOSE

The purpose of this lesson is to combine **analysis and synthesis** into an active thinking forum providing children with experiences to stimulate their **spatial intelligence**. In these activities, students will be introduced to *Max the Magician* who attempts to "fool our brains" through what our eyes perceive. This combines previously learned thinking skills in analyzing spatial relationships and reconstructing the parts into new wholes by making predictions. Students will be introduced to the following concepts:

— Visual thinking combines analysis of visual clues, logical deduction, flexibility of perspective, and fluency of thought.
— Shapes can be manipulated mentally, without concrete devices.
— Visual patterns are predictable.
— The eyes and the brain must work together to "think" about given information.

TEACHER MATERIALS

For projection:

— *Max the Magician* picture – a colorized Max is available on the CD
— *Max's Hatband*
— a set of pattern blocks (or a set for each student)
— *Rabbit Reversal*
— *Designer Details*

For duplication:

— *Max the Magician* story to read aloud
— *PETS™ Behavioral Checklist – Magician Thinking*
— picture of Max the Magician for each student to color
— class set of *Max's Magic Hat*
— class set of *Max's Hat Tricks*
— class set of *Make Max Reappear*

STUDENT MATERIALS

— crayons or colored pencils
— pencils
— glue
— scissors

LESSON PLAN

1. Introduce students to the concept of a *magician.* Magicians do not actually do magic. Instead they trick us by how we perceive or "see" things. Magicians are able to fool our brains into "seeing" what may not really be there. Magicians appear to pull a quarter out of a person's ear. The brain knows that the quarter was not in the ear, but it is still fooled into believing the trick. When using magician thinking, the brain must carefully interpret the information that the eyes see, or do not see, in order to reach reasonable solutions.

2. Read the story, *Max the Magician.* During the story, project *Max's Hatband* (be sure the triangles are colored green and the rectangles are colored red).

3. Have students make *Max's Magic Hat,* a pencil holder, which is the thinking skill memory trigger for this unit.

4. Using a predictable three-dimensional object, such as a teddy bear, help the students understand how to visualize the sides of the object that are not facing them. Hold the teddy bear close to your chest so that the students cannot see the back of it. It is preferable that the teddy bear have several distinguishing marks about it (a hat, a scarf, posable arms and legs, etc.). Ask the students to describe the bear to you. They will tell you about the bear's shape, color, hat, scarf, and so on. Ask students to tell you what the back of the bear looks like. Do the stripes on the hat go all the way around to the back? Is the scarf tied around the bear's neck, or is it stitched on at the sides?

5. Discuss how the students can "see" with their minds what they cannot see with their eyes. Help them understand that while they cannot be 100% certain that the back of this brown bear is not purple or whether or not it has a tail (since it is not a real bear, but a stuffed toy), their brains help them fill in the logical details about what they can expect. If the bear has posable arms and legs, ask the students to tell you how those arms and legs will look when the bear is turned around for them to see the back.

6. Project *Rabbit Reversal* and *Designer Details.* Work through them as a group. Although students should attempt to find the correct pairs mentally, the teacher may want to make extra copies, and cut out the shapes so that the answers from students can be tested.

CHALLENGE PAGES

Max's Hat Tricks   *Make Max Reappear*

7. Have students complete the challenge pages titled *Max's Hat Tricks* and *Make Max Reappear.* For diagnostic purposes, they need to be done independently in class.

ANSWER KEY

ANSWER KEY

Rabbit Reversal #2
Designer Details A-4, B-3, C-1, D-5, E-9, F-7, G-6, H-2, I-8

DIAGNOSTIC NOTES

During the lesson, look for students who visualize the manipulations of the shapes mentally without needing to manipulate the shapes manually. A checklist for the whole class lessons is provided. The following is a short summary of student behaviors to note:

GRASPS CONCEPTS – Look for students who quickly see the perceptions presented. If they need to be shown the "trick," such as turning a pattern block, note those students who remember that "trick" and will try it in other situations.

SEES INTERRELATIONSHIP OF CLUES – Look for students who use all available clues or ideas to figure out the pattern.

MANIPULATES SHAPES MENTALLY – Sometimes the teacher will be able to observe the students as they turn their heads or hands, trying to visualize or manipulate an object mentally.

DEFERS JUDGMENT – These are the students who will wait to answer rather than jumping to a wrong conclusion.

SEES ANSWERS INTUITIVELY – Look for students who seem to understand intuitively the visual patterns presented. They correctly identify the patterns without quite knowing how they got the answers.

IS TENACIOUS – In addition to working diligently to the end of the activities, look for students who want to work on visual thinking activities. An enthusiasm towards this type of problem usually indicates an ability to solve the problems.

RETAINS INFORMATION – When reviewing ideas from earlier lessons, look for students who clearly recall the concepts and then effectively apply them to the current lesson's activities. While many children may grasp concepts "in the moment" of the instructional lesson, these students exhibit the significant ability to retain and apply new learning across time.

Max's Hat Tricks and ***Make Max Reappear***
Look for students who:
- — solve the puzzles correctly.
- — redraw Max accurately.

MAX THE MAGICIAN

Today was a very special day in Crystal Pond Woods. Dudley the Detective, Sybil the Scientist, Yolanda the Yarnspinner, Isabel the Inventor, and Jordan the Judge were on their way to the beach along with all of the other animals from Crystal Pond Woods. Everyone was very excited because they knew that on this day they would see one of the best shows ever – Max the Magician was coming to the Woods!

Max is a rabbit, but a very unusual rabbit. Max was not born in Crystal Pond Woods like all the other animals. Max came out of a tall black hat, making Max a magical rabbit. His fur is white, his nose is pink, and he dresses in a beautifully patterned vest. Max has a way of looking at things that seems magical. He studies the **shapes** and **patterns** that are all around him.

Everyone quickly found seats as showtime approached. The lights dimmed, the audience hushed, and the curtain went up. The crowd cheered wildly as Max entered the stage. Max removed his tall, black hat and bowed deeply to the crowd. "Ladies and Gentlemen, welcome to the greatest show in the Woods."

Max set his tall, black hat on the table.

(At this time, project Max's Hatband.*)*

Max waved his right hand to the crowd and reached into his tall, black hat and pulled out a handful of brightly colored blocks.

(At this time, put some pattern blocks on the projector and/or give students some pattern blocks.)

Pointing to the pattern on the hatband of his tall, black hat, Max challenged the crowd, "Can you use these special pattern blocks and make the pattern on my hatband?"

The crowd was excited. All the animals of Crystal Pond Woods love challenges and Max always provides special challenges.

(Allow students time to try to figure out the pattern. The pattern is a green triangle and the red trapezoid, but the red trapezoid is turned so the view of the trapezoid is actually a red rectangle.)

The tension in the crowd was great as the minutes passed. Finally, Rascal Raccoon yelled, "I figured it out!"

Rascal Raccoon joined Max the Magician on stage and shared his solution with the crowd.

"I did not immediately see the answer because I laid all of my blocks flat on the ground. I knew the green triangle was part of the pattern, but I did not see a red rectangle. Because the red trapezoid was the only red block, I picked up the red trapezoid and looked at it from all different sides. While doing this, I noticed that when I hold it like this, *(hold the red trapezoid so that the rectangle side is viewed), it shows a rectangle.*"

The crowd showed its appreciation of Rascal Raccoon's solution by cheering wildly.

"We want more! We want more!" yelled the crowd.

"Okay, okay," answered Max the Magician. "My assistant, your teacher, has many more tricks to show you."

Max's
Hatband

Max's Magic Hat

1. Cut out the 2 hat pieces along the solid lines.
2. Clip the edge of the hat top along all of the dotted lines. Fold the flaps out.
3. Roll the hat top and glue over the shaded area. Glue the top to the bottom around the shaded inner circle.

MAX the Magician

Rabbit Reversal

Which of Max's pictures below is the same as the Max in the box — **but turned in a different direction?**

1

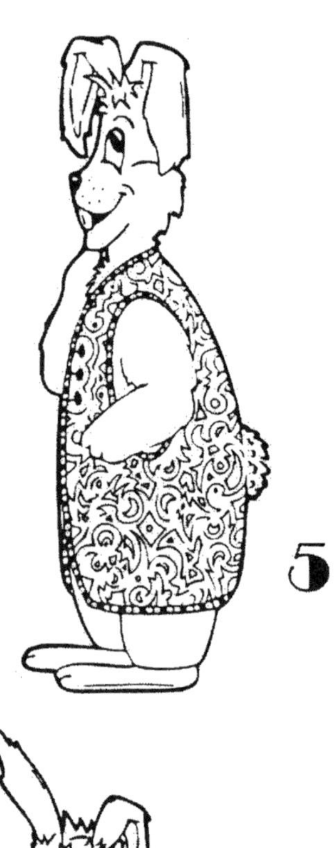

5

2

3

4

Designer Details

These designs are from Max's vest. Match each design with a letter to an identical shape with a number. Write the correct letter in each numbered shape.

A B C D

E F G H I

1 2 3 4 5

6 7 8 9

Name ______________________________

Max's Hat Tricks

Subtract the figures in each hat. Draw what's left. Here's how:

Name ______________________________

Make Max Reappear

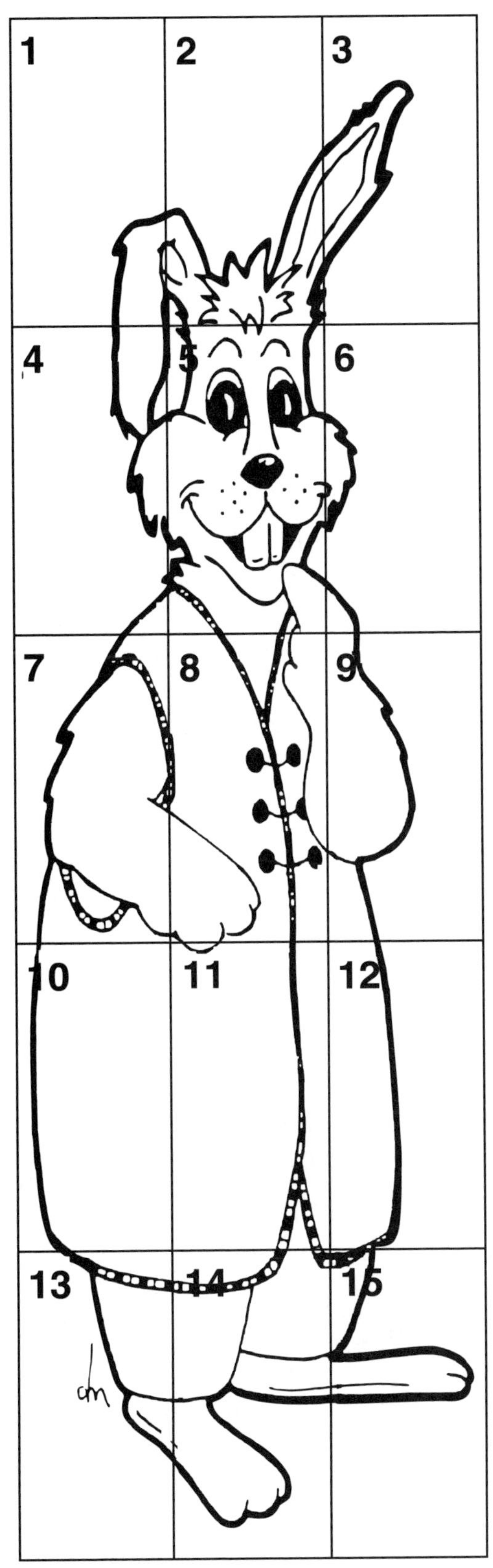

1	2	3
4	5	6
7	8	9
10	11	12
13	14	15

MAGICIAN THINKING WHOLE CLASS LESSON 2

PURPOSE

The purpose of this lesson is to review and reinforce the concepts presented in the previous lesson. Students will continue to practice their **visual/spatial perception** by analyzing patterns which repeat and extend and are completely predictable. Students will also create original patterns using their high-level visual thinking skills.

TEACHER MATERIALS

For duplication:

— *PETS™ Behavioral Checklist – Magician Thinking*
— class set of *Pattern Panels* OR a set of manipulatives, such as Unifix® cubes, for each student
— class set of *Hat Strings*

STUDENT MATERIALS

— crayons or colored pencils
— pencils
— glue
— scissors

LESSON PLAN

1. Review with students the concept of a *magician.* Magicians do not actually do magic. Instead they trick us by how we see or perceive things. During this unit, students are going to look at objects and study how they are perceived.

2. Each student will need a set of beads, Unifix® Cubes, Cuisenaire® rods, or other manipulatives suitable for creating patterns. *Pattern Panels* can be used in place of the manipulatives.

3. Using the manipulative, create a complicated, intricate pattern and ask the students to continue it. An example might be to create a stick of Unifix® Cubes or a string of beads using the following pattern: yellow, blue, yellow, blue, blue, yellow, blue, blue, blue, yellow, blue. The students should use their own Unfix® cubes to make the next ten steps in this pattern. The difficulty for the students is that they must begin their portion in the middle of the extending unit. Therefore, their stick or string should be blue, blue, blue, yellow, blue, blue, blue, blue, blue, yellow. Find someone with the correct

response and add theirs to your own pattern and help the class to see why this response continues your pattern.

4. A second, more intricate pattern may be red, white, red, red, white, green, red, red, red, white, white, green, green, 4 reds, 3 whites, 3 greens. Ask students to continue the pattern by creating the next 10 steps. The correct response will be 5 reds, 4 whites, 1 green. Students may have difficulty stopping in the middle of a unit. Encourage them to give you only the next 10 steps.

5. Discuss how to find a pattern. How does one know where the pattern begins and ends? This second pattern seems to have some irrelevant information at the beginning. Elicit that there are patterns where the unit *repeats* and those where the unit *extends.* The essence of the pattern is that it is *predictable.* The students must disregard the blocks at the beginning and look for the beginning of the portion they can predict.

CHALLENGE PAGE

Hat Strings

6. Give students the challenge page titled *Hat Strings* which is to be done independently in class. Tell the students that when they are finished they will cut the hats into five strips, horizontally across the page, and glue the strips end to end to create one long strip of hats.

7. Challenge the students to create a pattern to stump you by coloring the hats on the first four strips and leaving the last strip blank for you to figure out.

DIAGNOSTIC NOTES

During the lesson, look for students who visualize the manipulations of the shapes mentally without needing to manipulate the shapes manually. A checklist for the whole class lessons is provided. The following is a short summary of student behaviors to note:

GRASPS CONCEPTS – Look for students who recognize and predict the patterns, even if it is in the middle of a unit. Also look for students who design a complicated pattern which extends rather than repeats. Highest level thinkers will create patterns which extend in a predictable manner, rather than patterns which simply repeat, such as red, blue, red, blue, no matter how long the unit.

SEES THE INTERRELATIONSHIP OF CLUES – Look for students who use all available clues or ideas to figure out the pattern.

MANIPULATES SHAPES MENTALLY – Watch for students turning their heads or hands, trying to visualize or manipulate objects mentally.

DEFERS JUDGMENT – Look for students who wait to answer rather than jumping to a wrong conclusion.

SEES ANSWERS INTUITIVELY – Look for students who seem to understand intuitively the visual patterns presented. They correctly identify the patterns without quite knowing how they got the answers.

IS TENACIOUS – In addition to working diligently to the end of the activities, watch for students who want to work on visual thinking activities. An enthusiasm towards this type of problem often indicates an ability to solve the problems.

RETAINS INFORMATION – When reviewing ideas from earlier lessons, look for students who clearly recall the concepts and then effectively apply them to the current lesson's activities. While many children may grasp concepts "in the moment" of the instructional lesson, these students exhibit the significant ability to retain and apply new learning across time.

Hat Strings
Look for students who:

— create a predictable, repeating pattern.
— create a more challenging predictable, extending pattern.

NOTES

Name ______________________________

Pattern Panels

Name ______________________________

Hat Strings

Create a pattern using these hats.

MAGICIAN THINKING
SMALL GROUP
LESSON 1

PURPOSE

The purpose of this lesson is to provide further **visual/spatial** problem-solving through the **manipulation** of **symmetrical shapes.** Students will be challenged to arrange twenty-six pairs of symmetrical designs in a continuous pattern.

TEACHER MATERIALS

For duplication:

— *PETS™ Small Group Checklist* for each student

— *Max's Mirror Dominoes* for each student. If cut out and laminated ahead of time, these sets can be used repeatedly.

STUDENT MATERIALS

— scissors (only if students are cutting out their own dominoes)

LESSON PLAN

1. If sets of *Max's Mirror Dominoes* have not been prepared previously, students will need to start by cutting out their own sets.

2. Each end of a domino has a mirror image on the end of another domino. After choosing a domino with which to start, each student creates a domino train by matching up the mirror images on the dominoes.

3. If all the dominoes are matched correctly, the image on the end of the last domino placed will match up to the image at the beginning of the train.

4. Point out to students that when the mirror images are matched, each pair forms a *symmetrical* design.

DIAGNOSTIC NOTES

Look for students who:

— quickly and accurately select the right design from the pile.

— develop alternate strategies for solving the problem. For example, instead of looking only for the next match in order from beginning to end, a student will match pairs or triplets as he finds them making preliminary partial trains before ultimately combining them all together.

— realize that reversing a partial train may be necessary to make a match.

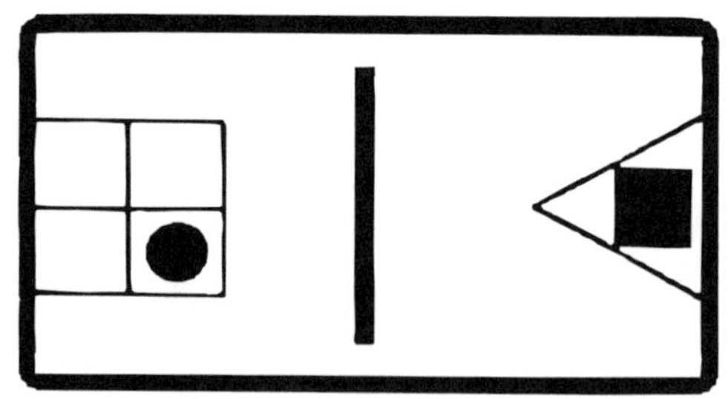

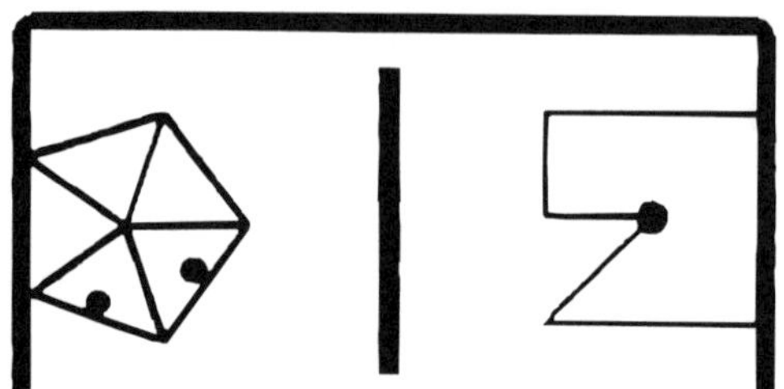

Max's Mirror Dominoes

Arrange the dominoes in a continuous pattern so that the design on the end of the last domino matches the beginning end of the first domino.

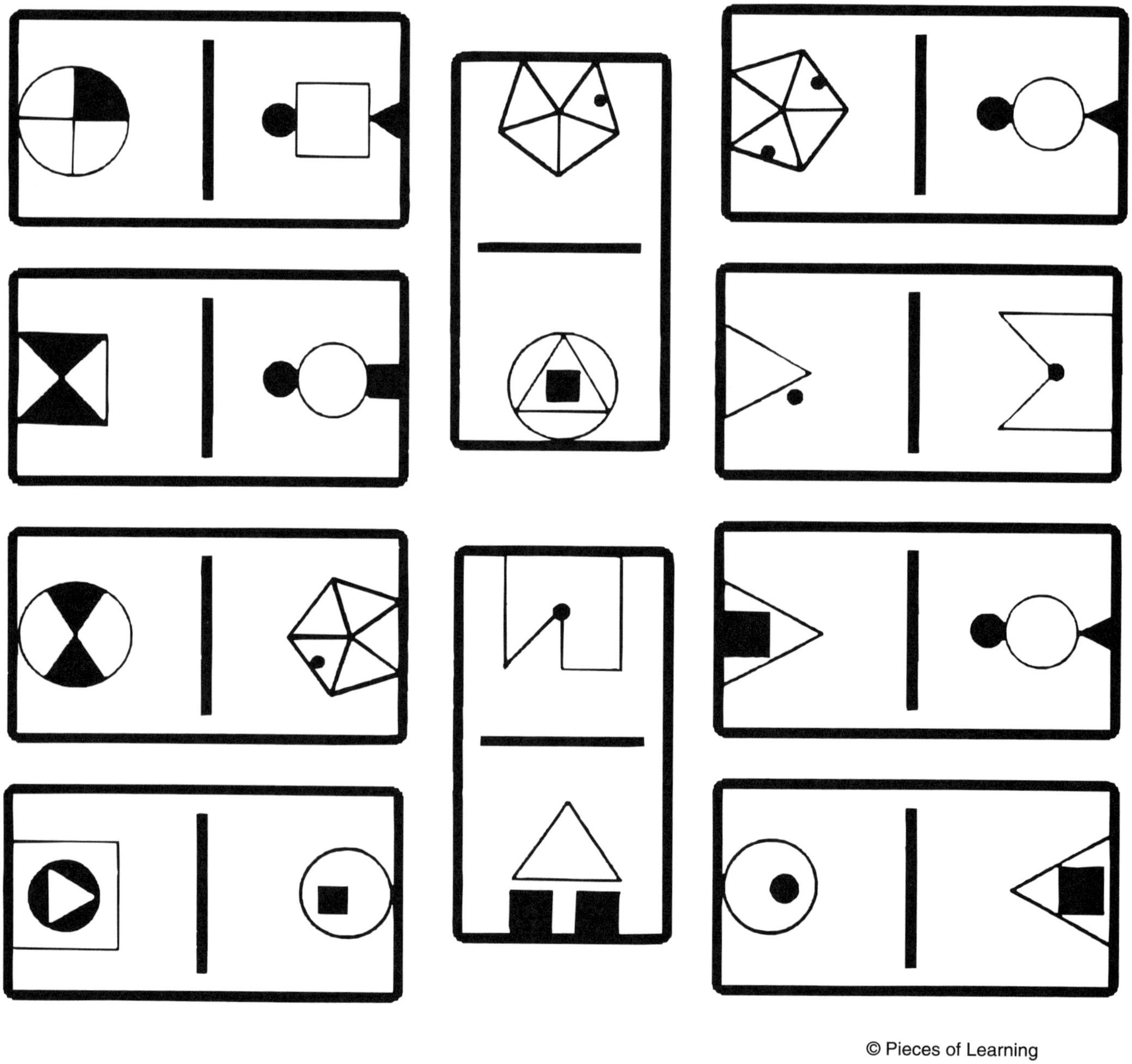

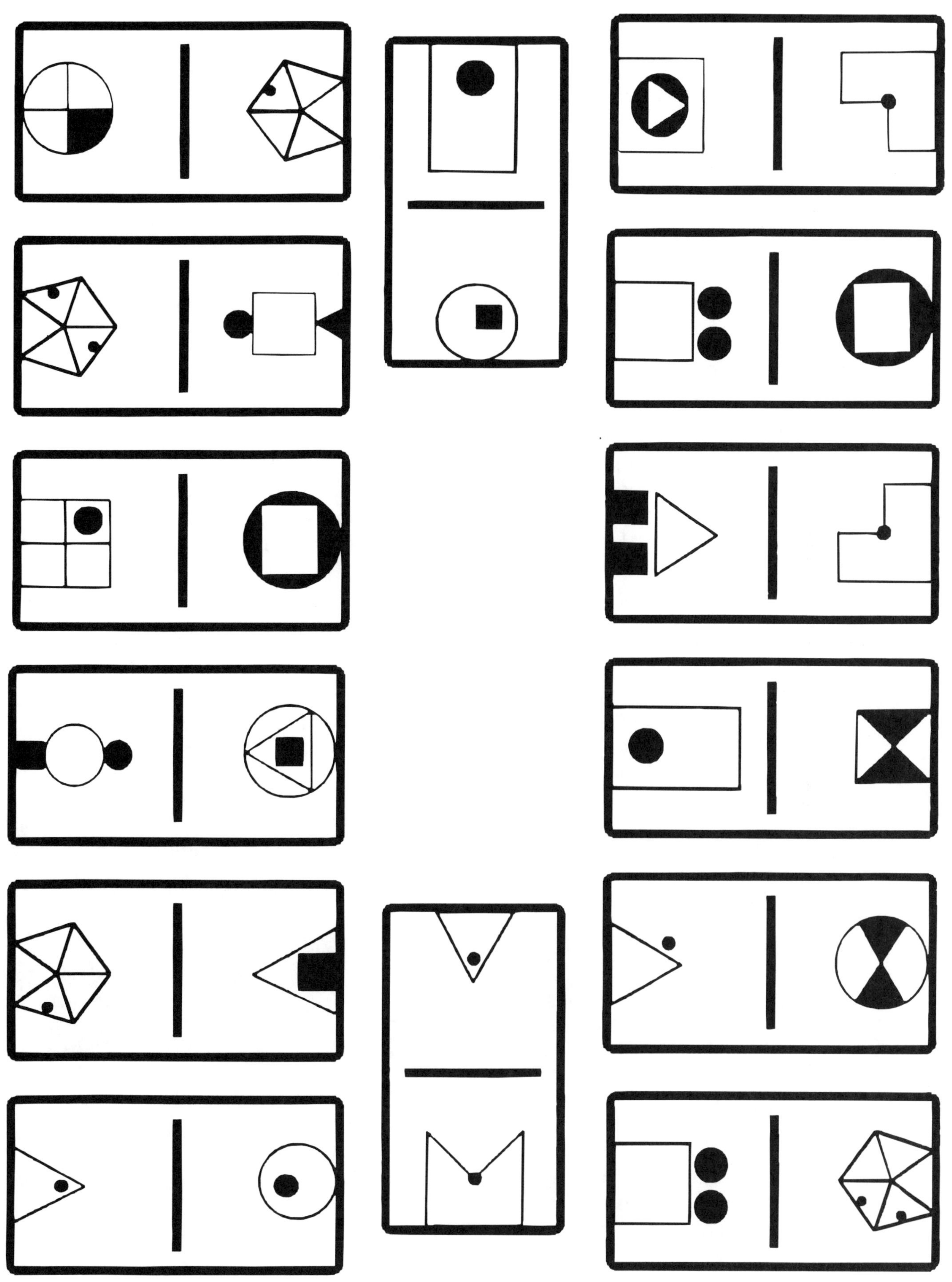

MAGICIAN THINKING SMALL GROUP LESSON 2

PURPOSE

The purpose of this lesson is to provide further **visual/spatial** problem-solving through the **manipulation** of **tangrams**. As students rotate the tangrams to their correct positions, they solve the puzzles.

TEACHER MATERIALS

For duplication:

— *PETS™ Small Group Checklist* for each student
— *Max's Magic Tangrams* for each student (commercial sets of plastic tangrams can also be used)
— *A Friend for Max/A Present for Max* and *A Tangram Bird/A Magic Hat* for each student. Laminate these to use with other groups.

STUDENT MATERIALS

— scissors (if students are cutting out their own tangrams)

LESSON PLAN

1. Explain to students that the puzzle pieces on *Max's Magic Tangrams* are the seven traditional tangram shapes. Have students cut out these pieces and put them together to make Max the Magician in a rectangular format.

2. Use the tangram pieces to solve these puzzles: *A Friend for Max, A Present for Max, A Tangram Bird,* and *A Magic Hat.* If the pictures of Max on the tangram shapes interfere with the problem-solving, have students turn the puzzle pieces over.

ANSWER KEY

DIAGNOSTIC NOTES

Look for students who:

— understand that different puzzle pieces can be used to cover the same area but in a different way. For example, the two small triangles can be used in the place of a square.
— "see" the relationships between the shapes and easily rotate, flip, or combine them to solve the puzzles.

Max's Magic Tangrams

Max's vest has many pockets. In one very special pocket are his tangram pieces. Max makes puzzles with his tangrams. Use the puzzle pieces to solve Max's shapes and pictures.

Begin by putting Max back together again. This puzzle will make a rectangle. Cut out puzzle pieces along the outside edges for the best fit.

Next, make a square with the two largest triangles. Now make a square the same size with all the other pieces.

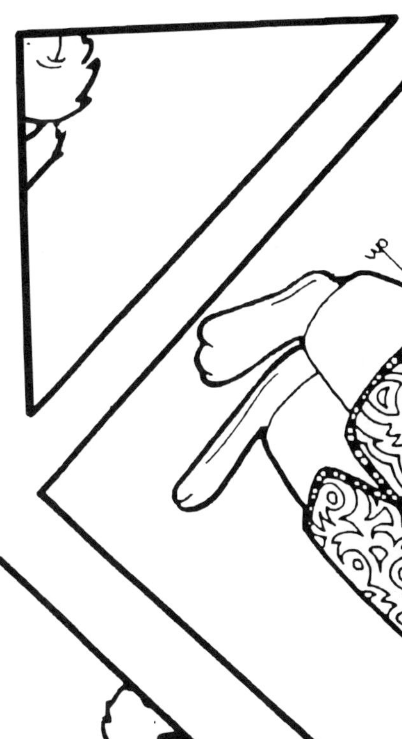

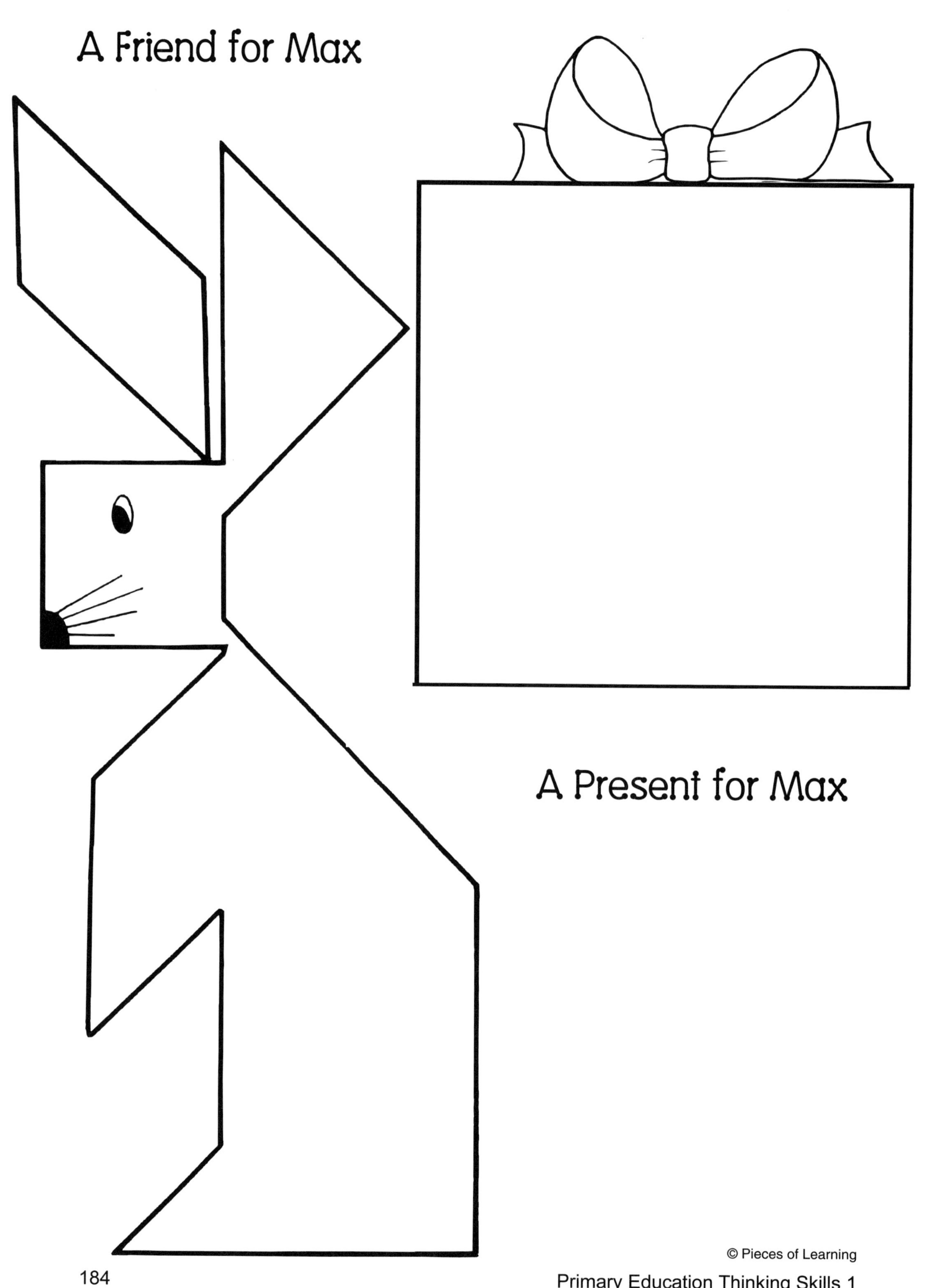
A Friend for Max
A Present for Max

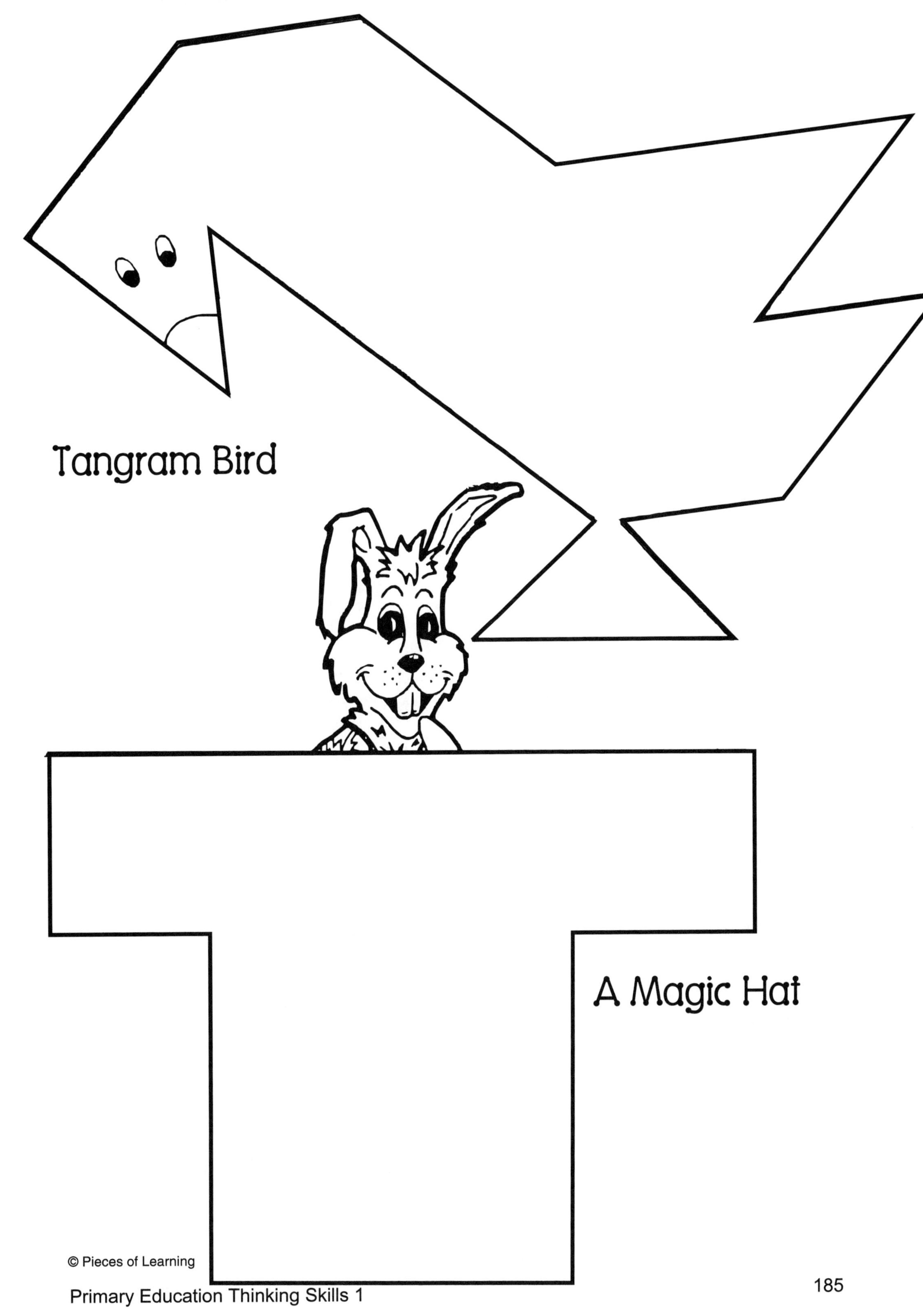
Tangram Bird
A Magic Hat

Ask me what I did in Thinking Skills today!
. . . looking for visual patterns . . .

Ask me what I did in Thinking Skills today!
. . . Looking for visual patterns . . .

Ask me what I did in Thinking Skills today!
. . . looking for visual patterns . . .

Ask me what I did in Thinking Skills today!
. . . looking for visual patterns . . .

Jordan the Judge

. . . Uses ***considerations*** . . . To find ***the best*** answer

Evaluative Thinking

List names of students as each behavior appears. **Add checkmarks** after name if behavior is repeated. **Use a different color** of ink or pencil for each whole group lesson.	**PETS™** **Behavioral Checklist** **Judge Thinking** (criteria-based evaluative thinking)	Teacher ________ Grade ______ Dates of whole group instruction: 1. _______ 2. _______

GRASPS CONCEPTS QUICKLY	**DRAWS VALID CONCLUSIONS BASED UPON CONSIDERATIONS** DEVELOPED IN THE LESSON
SUPPORTS RESPONSES LOGICALLY	**SEES MORE THAN ONE VIEWPOINT**
OFFERS UNIQUE CONSIDERATIONS AND/ OR **SOLUTIONS**	**IS TENACIOUS** IN APPROACH; WORKS DILIGENTLY TO THE END
RETAINS INFORMATION FROM PREVIOUS LESSONS	**PETS™ CLASSWORK** INDICATES AN OUTSTANDING ABILITY TO USE THIS THINKING SKILL

I see these behaviors in these students regularly during class time as well:	These students did not stand out during the PETS™ lessons, but I see these behaviors during regular class time:	Notes:

DIAGNOSTIC NOTES • JUDGE THINKING

GRASPS CONCEPTS QUICKLY • *uses considerations to eliminate choices* • *offers lots of ideas for factual measurable/observable considerations* • *uses considerations to make valid choices*	**DRAWS VALID CONCLUSIONS BASED UPON CONSIDERATIONS** DEVELOPED IN THE LESSON • *applies valid considerations accurately to narrow the field of choices regardless of personal preferences*
SUPPORTS RESPONSES LOGICALLY • *states considerations used in determining solution choice* • *supports considerations by offering ways of observing or measuring them*	**SEES MORE THAN ONE VIEWPOINT** • *sees the viewpoints of others* • *develops considerations from other viewpoints*
OFFERS UNIQUE CONSIDERATIONS AND/ OR **SOLUTIONS** • *offers valid considerations not previously stated*	**IS TENACIOUS** IN APPROACH; WORKS DILIGENTLY TO THE END • *works diligently to conclusion* • *will NOT give up*
RETAINS INFORMATION FROM PREVIOUS LESSONS • *shares knowledge accurately during review* • *applies knowledge during activities*	**PETS™ CLASSWORK** INDICATES AN OUTSTANDING ABILITY TO USE THIS THINKING SKILL • *seatwork and/or challenge papers are exceptionally well done*

I see these behaviors in these students regularly during class time as well:	These students did not stand out during the PETS™ lessons, but I see these behaviors during regular class time:	Notes:
• *normally great evaluative thinkers*	• *normally great evaluative thinkers who "hid out" during the PETS™ lesson*	• *absentees* • *new students*

- *be generous — more inclusive than exclusive*
- *names can go in more than one box per answer*
- *be sure to add ✓s after names for multiple answers*
- *be sure to use different colors for each whole group lesson*

JUDGE THINKING
WHOLE CLASS
LESSON 1

PURPOSE

The purpose of this lesson is to introduce students to **evaluative thinking.** There are three types of evaluative thinking: criterion-based evaluation, value judgments, and judicial evaluation. This lesson deals with *criterion-based evaluation.* Through the story of Jordan the Judge, students will be encouraged to base their decisions (or choices) on factual, measurable or observable *considerations* (or criteria). The students will be introduced to the following concepts:

— Decisions are based on valid factual, observable or measurable considerations, not on opinions.
— When a choice must be made, considerations help guide students to the "best" solution when there is not one "right" answer.

TEACHER MATERIALS

For projection:

— *Jordan the Judge* picture – a colorized Jordan is available on the CD
— *Yolanda's List of Things to Buy*
— *Brainstorming Considerations*

For duplication:

— *Jordan the Judge* story to read aloud
— *PETS™ Behavioral Checklist – Judge Thinking*
— picture of Jordan the Judge for each student to color
— class set of *Jordan's Gavel* (OR straight pretzels and marshmallows for gavels)
— class set of *A Pet for You*

STUDENT MATERIALS

— crayons or colored pencils
— pencils
— scissors
— glue

LESSON PLAN

1. Introduce students to the concept of a *judge.* Ask students if they know any judges. Give students the opportunity to describe what judges do. Discuss that judges are not only in a courtroom but there are also judges at contests.

2. Tell students that today they are going to meet *Jordan the Judge* who uses *considerations* to help him solve his problems. Project the picture of Jordan. Students may color their pictures of Jordan at this time or after reading the story.

3. Read the *Jordan the Judge* story.

4. Review with students that Jordan the Judge helps people make decisions when there is a choice to be made (when there is not one "right" answer). He always begins by asking, *"What are the considerations?"* Once he has thought about all of the considerations, Jordan bangs his gavel and announces the "best" choice.

5. Have students cut out and color their gavels, the memory trigger for this unit. An alternative to the paper gavel is making gavels from skinny straight pretzels and air-puffed marshmallows. Students can quietly bang these gavels for the rest of the lesson!

6. Project *Brainstorming Considerations.* Ask the students what they would want to consider <u>before</u> buying new gym shoes or choosing a game to play or deciding on what to eat for a snack. To be valid, their considerations must be factual – not just their opinions! These considerations need to be observable or measurable. Nor are students to jump ahead and announce what their choice might be. That is not the purpose of this activity – keep the focus on determining what considerations are important to them personally in the decision-making process.

For example, when considering a pair of gym shoes, "Are they cool?" or "Do I like them?" are not acceptable considerations. What is "cool"? How do you recognize "cool"? What does "like" mean? In these instances, tell students that more information is needed. Exactly what makes gym shoes cool that you can check out? What would you see that makes the gym shoes likable? "Do they have polka dots on them?" or "Are they my favorite color blue?" or "Are they high-tops?" are all acceptable considerations as they can be observed and validated.

Although not a requisite approach, encourage students to pose their considerations as questions. For example, when considering what game to play, these questions are valid considerations: "Do most of my friends like to play this game?" or "Can we finish this game in an hour?" Both are measurable considerations – note that polling how many people like a game is different than simply stating that you like it.

CHALLENGE PAGE

A Pet for You

7. Distribute the challenge page which is to be done independently while at school. Read the instructions aloud, making sure that everyone understands them. Remind them that there is not one "right" answer here – they just need to be sure that their considerations support their final choice!

DIAGNOSTIC NOTES

A checklist for the whole class lessons is provided. The following is a short summary of what student behaviors to note when thinking like a judge:

GRASPS CONCEPTS – Look for students who quickly understand the concept of using considerations to eliminate choices and make a decision.

DRAWS VALID CONCLUSIONS BASED ON CONSIDERATIONS – Look for students who accurately apply valid considerations in order to narrow the field of many choices regardless of their own personal preferences.

SUPPORTS RESPONSES LOGICALLY – Look for students who state their positions and can follow-up their positions with logical reasoning.

SEES MORE THAN ONE VIEWPOINT – Look for students who see the issue from another's viewpoint. Especially notable are any students who develop valid, factual measurable or observable considerations from the other viewpoint on their own.

OFFERS UNIQUE CONSIDERATIONS AND/OR SOLUTIONS – Look for students who provide considerations that have not been previously stated. These considerations may even surprise the teacher.

IS TENACIOUS – In addition to working diligently to the end of the activities, watch for students who want to work on evaluative-type activities. An enthusiasm toward this type of thinking often indicates an ability to use it well.

RETAINS INFORMATION – When reviewing ideas from earlier lessons, look for students who clearly recall the concepts and then effectively apply them to the current lesson's activities. While many children may grasp concepts "in the moment" of the instructional lesson, these students exhibit the significant ability to retain and apply new learning across time.

A Pet for You

Look for students who:

— create valid factual, measurable or observable considerations (or criteria).
— apply their considerations to the decision-making process effectively.

NOTES

JORDAN THE JUDGE

Yolanda the Yarnspinner and Rosalyn Robin were very excited one fine sunny day in Crystal Pond Woods. Yolanda had some extra money to spend. She had fifteen dollars to buy herself something special.

"Rosalyn Robin," sighed Yolanda. "There are so many wonderful things I want to buy! I can't decide on what would be the best thing to get with my money. What do you think?"

"I think we need to go visit Jordan the Judge," suggested Rosalyn. "He is always helping people with tough decisions so they make the **best choice.**"

Jordan is the judge for Crystal Pond Woods. His courtroom is a very special place. He sits at the front of the courtroom, high above everyone else. He has a gavel that he uses to get the court's attention before announcing his decision.

Jordan always tells the animals how important it is to base their choices and decisions on facts – on things that can be seen or measured. When one of the animals is having a hard time making a decision, Jordan will ask, **"What are your considerations?"** Then he listens to and thinks carefully about all the considerations. After arriving at the **best** answer in light of **these** considerations, Jordan bangs his gavel and announces his decision.

Yolanda and Rosalyn arrived at Jordan's courtroom to discover that it was very busy. They had to wait awhile until it was their turn. Jordan the Judge then said, "Good afternoon, ladies, what can I help you with today?"

"Well, Jordan the Judge," began Yolanda, "I have fifteen dollars to spend, and I can't decide how to spend it. Here is a list of all the wonderful things I would like to buy!" Yolanda handed Jordan the list and he read it aloud.

(Project Yolanda's List of Things to Buy *so students can follow along.)*

"You would like a black purse, a computer, a brown coat, a gray hat, a vase, a book of poems, a pair of red mittens, an orange scarf, a pair of black earrings, a brown sweater, and a red dress. Hmmm, I see that since any of these things would make a very good choice, there is *not* one right answer here – so to help you make the **best choice**, Yolanda, **what are your considerations?**"

"Well," replied Yolanda, "I have only fifteen dollars."

"That helps," said Jordan. "We can begin by eliminating all the items on your list that cost more than fifteen dollars."

(Discuss with students the items to be eliminated from the list because they are likely to cost more than fifteen dollars. Cross them off the list as students suggest them. Be sure that students are only considering the cost at this time.)

"OK, Yolanda," said Jordan the Judge, looking at the list that still had several items on it. "Do you have any other considerations?"

"Actually I do," continued Yolanda. "I know I want to buy something that will keep me warm in the winter."

"Well, well, that seems clear enough," Jordan responded. "Now we can eliminate all the items on your list that will not keep you warm."

(Now discuss with students which items should be eliminated from the list based solely on this new consideration. Cross them off the list.)

"We still haven't reached *one best choice* yet, Yolanda. Any further considerations?" questioned Jordan in commanding tones.

"Well, yes," answered Yolanda thoughtfully. "I love colorful words! So I think I should buy something really colorful!"

(Now discuss with students the items that should be eliminated based solely on the color consideration.)

"In that case, there are still two possibilities left, Yolanda – you can buy the pair of red mittens or the orange scarf. Would there be another consideration to keep in mind?" inquired Jordan.

Rosalyn Robin looked at Yolanda and then a smile broke out on her face. "Of course there is!" Rosalyn cried. "Yolanda is a spider! She has eight arms! A *pair* of mittens won't be enough to keep her warm!"

Jordan banged his gavel and proudly announced, "Then the **best** decision seems very clear. Buy the colorful orange scarf, Yolanda, that you can wrap all around yourself to stay warm throughout the winter. Case dismissed!"

Yolanda's List of Things to Buy

black purse

computer

brown coat

gray hat

vase

book of poems

pair of red mittens

orange scarf

black earrings

brown sweater

red dress

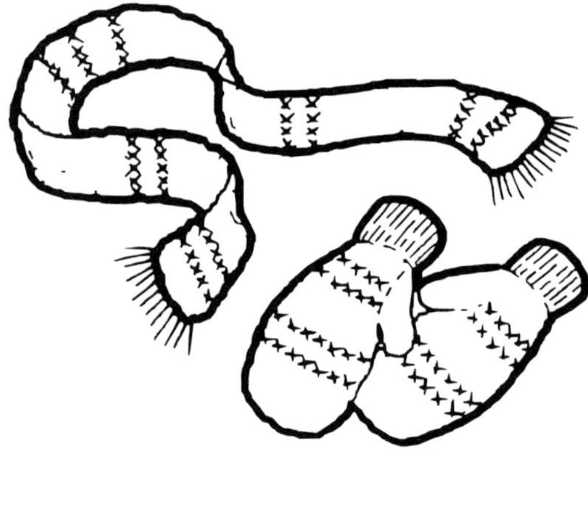

Jordan's Gavel

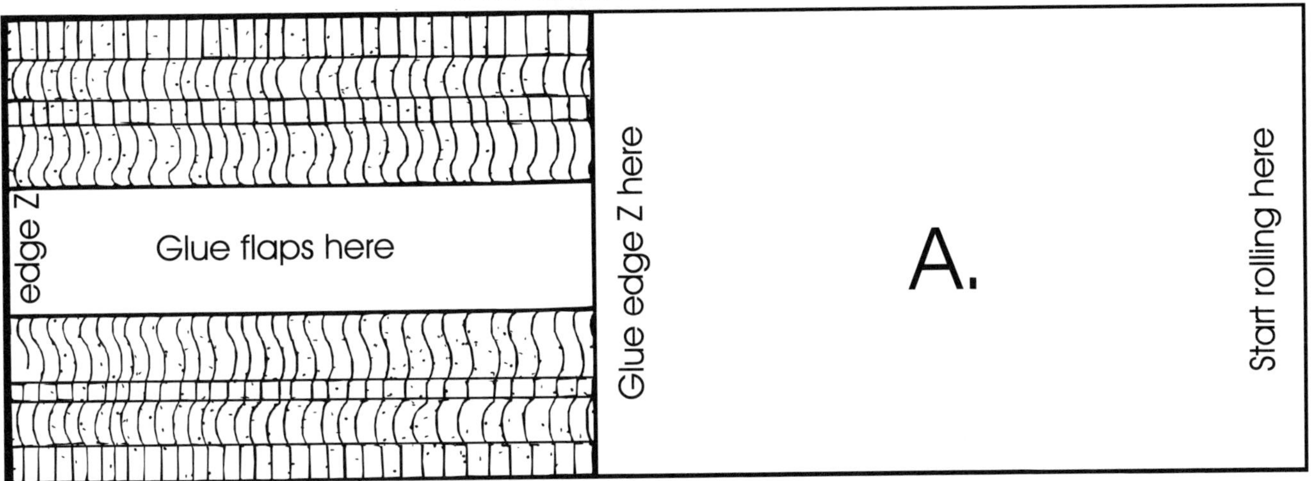

1. Cut out the 2 pieces (A, B) along the heavy, dark lines.
2. Roll up piece A and glue it closed (glue sticks best).
3. Fold piece B flat over and over along the dotted lines and glue it closed.
4. Fold out the flaps on piece B to form a Y.
5. Insert the roll into the Y formed by the flaps, lining up the flaps with the center channel. Overlap and glue the flaps around the roll.

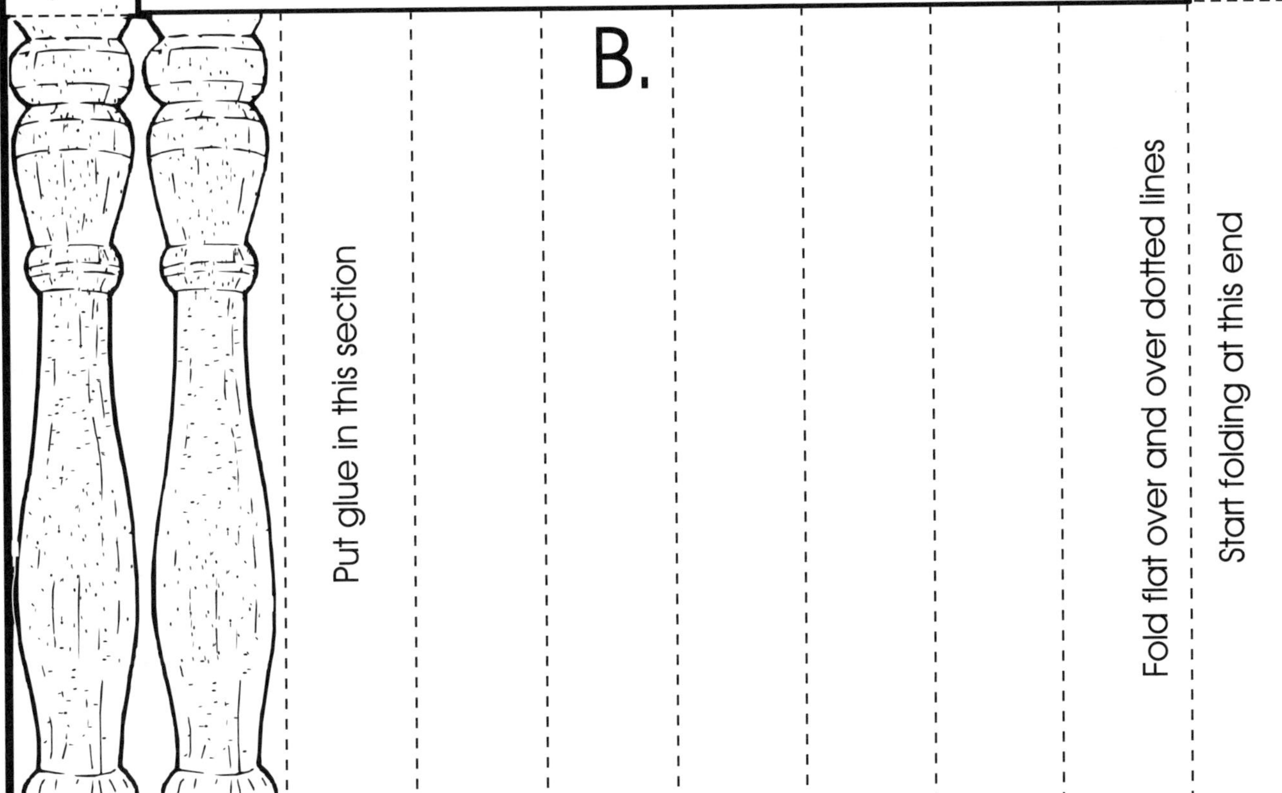

Brainstorming Considerations

What do you think about, or **consider**, when you have to make a decision? What questions do you ask yourself?

What **considerations** would help you make the **best** choice?

Brainstorm considerations that would help you make these decisions:

1. Shall I buy this pair of gym shoes?

1. ______________________________

____

2. ______________________________

____

3. ______________________________

____

4. ______________________________

____

2. What game do I want to play?

1. ______________________________

2. ______________________________

3. ______________________________

4. ______________________________

3. What shall I eat for a snack?

1. ______________________________
____

2. ______________________________
____

3. ______________________________
____

4. ______________________________
____

Name ______________________________

A Pet for You

Your parents have said you can choose a new pet!

Start with these 3 considerations. Read them carefully. Check either YES or NO.

YES		NO
☐	Do I have a fence around my yard?	☐
☐	Is anyone home during the day at my house?	☐
☐	Is anyone at home allergic to pet hair?	☐

What are some other things that you need to think about? I want a pet that:

1. ______________________________

2. ______________________________

3. ______________________________

Using these considerations, what's the BEST new pet for you? Draw it.

My new pet is a:

____

JUDGE THINKING
WHOLE CLASS
LESSON 2

PURPOSE

The purpose of this lesson is to introduce students to another way to **collect factual, observable or measurable information** to use in the decision-making process. The students will collect facts from the story ***Ira Sleeps Over*** on a T-chart. Students will learn that:

— The T-chart is useful for collecting decision-making information.
— The number of facts and the importance of the facts on one side of the T-chart should help in the evaluative process of making the best choice.

TEACHER MATERIALS

For projection:

— *Should Ira Take His Bear?*

For duplication:

— *PETS™ Behavioral Checklist – Judge Thinking*
— class set of *What Should We Buy?*

— one copy of the story ***Ira Sleeps Over*** by Bernard Waber to read aloud

STUDENT MATERIALS

— pencils

LESSON PLAN

1. Review with students the key ideas related to *Jordan the Judge*. Remind students that a judge helps people make decisions by asking, "What are the considerations?" When a judge has thought about all of the *considerations,* he bangs the gavel and announces the best solution.

2. Introduce the story ***Ira Sleeps Over*** by explaining to students that they are going to hear a story about Ira. Ira has an important decision to make. As the story is read, the class will make a list of what Ira considers when making his decision. Explain to students that in order to organize the considerations, they are going to use a T-chart. It is called a T-chart because of its shape. Project *Should Ira Take His Bear?*

3. Read the story to the students, pointing out Ira's dilemma – should he or should he not take his teddy bear to his very first sleep-over at his friend's house? As different considerations are introduced in the story, list them on the T-chart, *Should Ira Take His Bear?* Ask students whether each new fact is a reason for Ira to take his bear or not to take his bear to Reggie's house. Here are some possibilities:

On the "take the bear" side:

1. Ira has never slept without his teddy bear before.
2. Reggie is planning to tell scary ghost stories.
3. Reggie has his own bear, and it has a baby name, too.

On the "leave the bear" side:

1. Reggie will laugh and say Ira is a baby.
2. Reggie will laugh and say "Tah-Tah" is a baby name.

4. Discuss with students the T-chart. Ask students which side has more reasons. Discuss with students whether or not any of the considerations is more important than the others. When making a decision, some considerations are more important than others and therefore carry more weight. In the case of Ira, not only were there more "take the bear" considerations, but the most important consideration, #3, is also on the "take the bear" side. Ira should definitely have chosen to take his teddy bear, and Jordan the Judge is satisfied that Ira has decided wisely.

CHALLENGE PAGE

What Should We Buy?

5. Distribute the challenge page *What Should We Buy?* and read the introduction aloud to the class. As a group, brainstorm a list of things for your classroom on which they would like to spend the money. Determine the most popular idea and have <u>everyone</u> list that as Idea #1. Ideas #2 and #3 are student choice, either from the brainstormed list or something else a student wants for the classroom. Have students write each idea from the list in the appropriate numbered box – #1 in the box on side one; #2 and #3 in the boxes on side two.

As a group, work through Idea #1 (which is the same for everyone in the class). Brainstorm and list at least two YES considerations and two NO considerations so that students have a feel for analyzing their considerations and using a T-chart.

The individual challenge work is side two of *What Should We Buy?* This side needs to be done independently in class. Each student has to brainstorm both YES and NO considerations for the things that she thought would be good choices for your classroom.

Before they turn in their challenge pages, remind students to put a big star by the one choice that, based on the considerations listed on their T-charts, appears to be the best buy for your classroom.

DIAGNOSTIC NOTES

A checklist for the whole class lessons is provided. The following is a short summary of what student behaviors to note when thinking like a judge:

GRASPS CONCEPTS – Look for students who quickly determine which facts from the story are pertinent in Ira's decision-making and on which side of the T-chart they belong.

DRAWS VALID CONCLUSIONS BASED ON CONSIDERATIONS – Look for students who see that the T-chart information comprises the criteria for the decision-making process, regardless of their own personal feelings about teddy bears.

SUPPORTS RESPONSES LOGICALLY – Look for students who state their positions and can follow-up their positions with logical reasoning.

SEES MORE THAN ONE VIEWPOINT – Look for students who see the issue from another's viewpoint and students who understand how the decision may be different depending on the character making the decision.

OFFERS UNIQUE CONSIDERATIONS AND/OR SOLUTIONS – Look for students who offer considerations related to, but not directly from, the story.

IS TENACIOUS – In addition to working diligently to the end of the activities, watch for students who want to work on evaluative-type activities. An enthusiasm toward this type of thinking often indicates an ability to use it well.

RETAINS INFORMATION – When reviewing ideas from earlier lessons, look for students who clearly recall the concepts and then effectively apply them to the current lesson's activities. While many children may grasp concepts "in the moment" of the instructional lesson, these students exhibit the significant ability to retain and apply new learning across time.

What Should We Buy?

Look for students who:

— create valid factual, measurable or observable considerations (or criteria).

— apply their considerations to the decision-making process effectively.

NOTES

Should Ira Take His Bear?

What are Ira's **considerations?**

take the bear	leave the bear

Name ______________________

What Should We Buy ???

There's a lot of money in our class treasury from all our fundraisers. It's time to buy something very special for our classroom — what will it be?

Brainstorm 3 things we might buy for our classroom:

Idea #1: ______________________

Idea #2: ______________________

Idea #3: ______________________

But do we *really* want any of these wonderful things?
Let's look at some YES considerations and some NO considerations.

Put **Idea #1** in this box:

1. [ ]

YES considerations	NO considerations
1. ______________________	1. ______________________
______________________	______________________
2. ______________________	2. ______________________
______________________	______________________
3. ______________________	3. ______________________
______________________	______________________

Name ______________________

Put **Idea #2** in this box:

2. [ ]

YES considerations	NO considerations
1. ______________	1. ______________
2. ______________	2. ______________
3. ______________	3. ______________

Put **Idea #3** in this box:

3. [ ]

YES considerations	NO considerations
1. ______________	1. ______________
2. ______________	2. ______________
3. ______________	3. ______________

What's the **best** thing to spend our money on?
Put a big star next to it!!

JUDGE THINKING
SMALL GROUP
LESSON 1

PURPOSE

The purpose of this lesson is to reinforce and extend the evaluative thinking concepts presented during the whole class lessons. Students will be **applying factual, observable or measurable considerations** when making decisions and supporting their points of view.

TEACHER MATERIALS

For duplication:

— *PETS™ Small Group Checklist* for each student
— a laminated set of the *Paint a Picture Card Set*
— a laminated set of the *Build a Doghouse Card Set*
— a laminated set of the *Bake a Cake Card Set*
— a set of laminated instruction cards for *Jordan's Notable Necessities*

LESSON PLAN

1. Review with students the characteristics of *thinking like a judge*. In order to make the best decision, a judge will ask, "What are the considerations?" These considerations should be based on *factual, observable or measurable information.*

2. Choose one of the decks to demonstrate the lesson with the entire group. Spread the eight cards on the table and the instruction card from *Jordan's Notable Necessities.*

3. In the form of a class discussion, ask students to select the six items they need most to accomplish the task. Allow students time to discuss each item and its relevance to the task. When the group has selected six items, have them prioritize the cards, ranking the items from most important to least important. Encourage factual criteria as support for their choices, and allow good-natured debate and disagreement. Encourage students to support their ideas and persuade the group toward their points of view. Throughout this activity, it is the criteria which are important, not the actual selections. The teacher should never allow his own opinion to enter into the discussion; rather, students' points of view should be validated as long as their support and criteria are reasonable.

4. After the entire group has participated in the guided evaluative activity, divide the group into two smaller groups and give each group another set of the cards. Groups will have different task cards at this point. Have each group work independently work through the same evaluative process as before, but without any teacher guidance. The

teacher's role is simply to monitor discussions and listen for students who are capable of making evaluations based on sound factual, observable or measurable criteria.

DIAGNOSTIC NOTES

Look for students who:
- — apply their own factual considerations.
- — make valid evaluations.
- — support their points of view.
- — see other viewpoints.

NOTES

Jordan's Notable Necessities

Using the appropriate deck of cards, select and rate the 6 most needed items to accomplish these 3 tasks.

Build a Doghouse

1. Select the 6 items from the set of 8 that you feel are most needed to build a doghouse.

2. Rank these 6 items from most important to least important.

3. Explain your choices and rating.

Bake a Cake

1. Select the 6 items from the set of 8 that you feel are most needed to bake a cake.

2. Rank these 6 items from most important to least important.

3. Explain your choices and rating.

Paint a Picture

1. Select the 6 items from the set of 8 that you feel are most needed to paint a picture.

2. Rank these 6 items from most important to least important.

3. Explain your choices and rating.

Paint a Picture Card Set

bowl of fruit

pencil

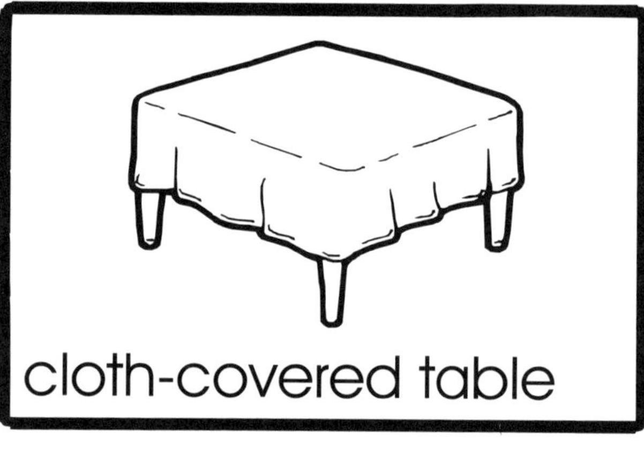
cloth-covered table

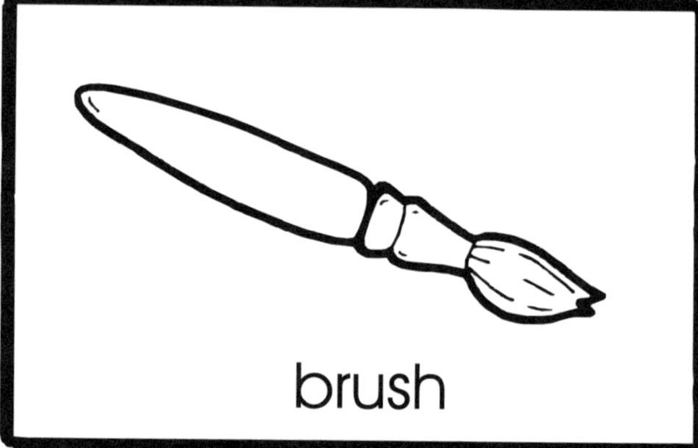
brush

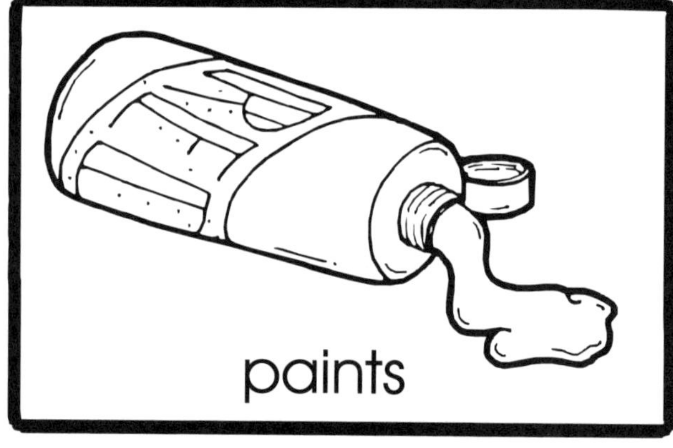
paints

paper

water

easel

Build a Doghouse Card Set

wood

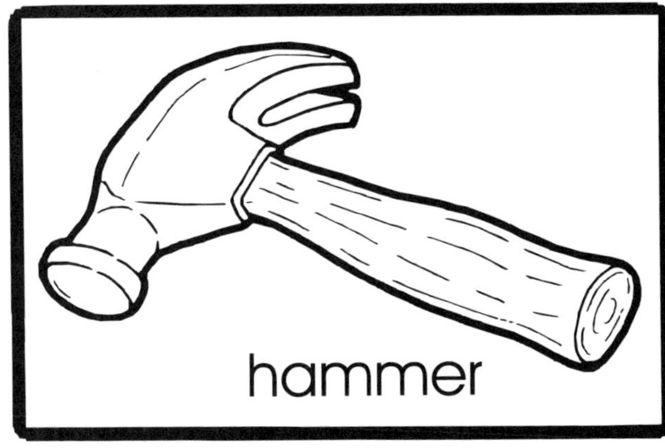

hammer

nails

book

paint

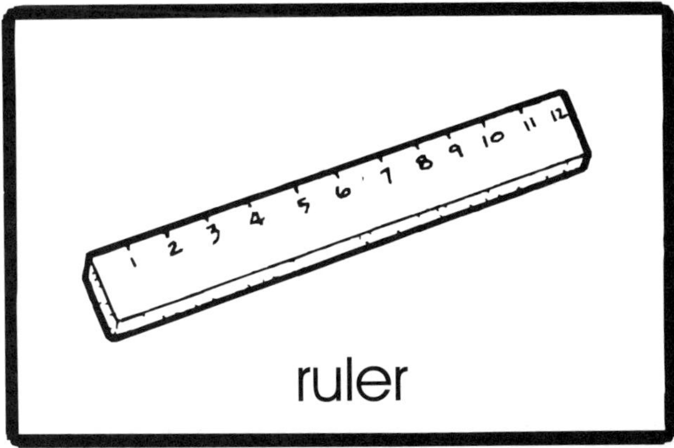

ruler

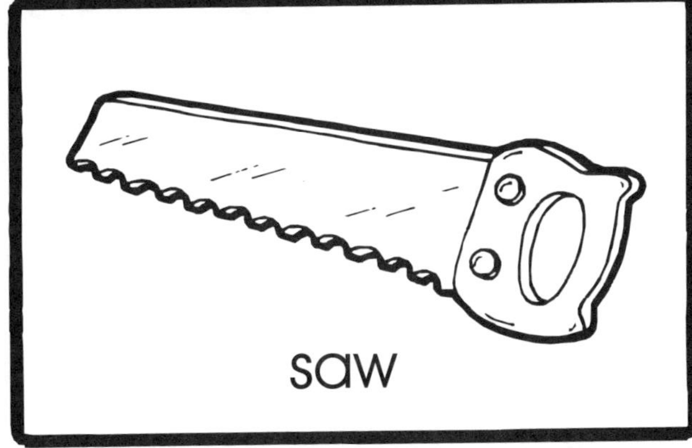

saw

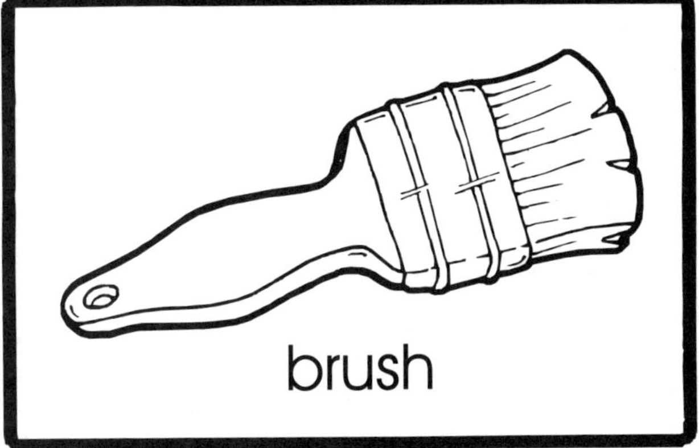

brush

Bake a Cake Card Set

JUDGE THINKING
SMALL GROUP
LESSON 2

PURPOSE

The purpose of this lesson is to reinforce the use of **factual, observable or measurable considerations** when making decisions. Students will be supporting their choices with specific considerations.

TEACHER MATERIALS

For duplication:

— *PETS™ Small Group Checklist* for each student
— *A Very Buggy BZZZZZness* chart for each student
— *A Very Buggy BZZZZZness* bugs for each student

— an 8.5" x 11" sheet of white paper for each student
— an 11" x 17" sheet of colored construction paper for each student
— chart paper

STUDENT MATERIALS

— crayons or colored pencils
— pencils
— scissors
— glue

LESSON PLAN

1. Review with students the characteristics of *thinking like a judge*. Explain to students that in this lesson they are going to use the considerations they have about bugs to decide what kinds of bugs are going to live in their world.

2. Brainstorm types of bugs with the class. Record the list on chart paper.

The term "bugs" is used here deliberately to allow students to include insects (3 body parts, 6 legs), arachnids (such as spiders, daddy longlegs, mites, and ticks that have 2 body parts and 8 legs), and some arthropods (such as centipedes and millipedes that have long multi-segmented bodies and many legs). Insects are classified according to the physical characteristics of the adult form which explains why many-legged caterpillars are still considered to be insects. Slugs (terrestrial mollusks) and worms (annelids) would not be included.

Some specific points about bugs included in this lesson:

Little black ants
- most abundant of all land animals
- great food source for birds and other animals
- destroy other pests and insects
- scavenge human food
- some specialized ants: harvest seeds, raise fungus for good, eat leaves cut from plants, tunnel in wood, kill and eat nesting birds

Swallowtail butterflies
- largest and most gorgeous butterfly
- feed on leaves

Ground beetles
- colorful
- known as caterpillar hunters
- eat lots of pests

House flies
- feed by lapping up liquids
- spread disease

Orb weaver spiders
- eat insects
- make a spiraling orb-shaped web each night,
  - the old web is replaced with a new one
  - spun in complete darkness by touch alone
  - takes about one hour
  - it will hold 4000 times the spider's own weight
  - uses about 63 feet of silk
- each kind of orb weaver spider spins its own kind of web
  - from the moment it leaves its egg it knows how to spin a certain pattern

Honey bees
- most important pollinator
- make honey
- use bee "language" a complex direction-giving dance

Dragonflies
- eat flying insects including mosquitoes

Crickets
- eat plants, pests, blankets, sweaters, baskets
- make chirping sounds by rubbing wings together

Ladybug beetles
- eat aphids and other pests

Firefly beetles
- create light through a chemical reaction in abdomen
- blink light to attract a mate

3. Brainstorm "good" things (they pollinate flowers) and "bad" things (they sting) about bugs. See the list of some things to consider for each bug on the previous page. Use a T-chart to record student ideas on the chart paper.

4. Give a copy of the chart, *A Very Buggy BZZZZZness,* to each student. Have students follow these steps:
  — Go through the list of bugs.
  — Check "yes" for each bug they want to keep in their world.
  — Check "no" for each bug they would like to eliminate from their world.
  — Write the factual consideration on which the decision to check "yes" or "no" was based in the larger box by the checkmark. For example, a student not wanting to have crickets around might support this decision by stating, "They make too much noise." Students may list as many considerations for each bug as will fit. Remember – "I like them" and "I don't like them" are not factual, observable or measurable considerations.

5. Give each student a piece of white paper. Have students draw their choice of a picture of the world or some special place in the world on it.

6. Give each student a copy of *A Very Buggy BZZZZZness* bugs. Students may cut out and glue onto their drawings of the world (or a special place in the world) only the bugs that they checked "yes."

7. Give each student a piece of construction paper. Tell students to fold their sheets in half and then open them back up. Instruct them to glue their drawing on one side of the fold line in the middle of the construction paper and then glue their *A Very Buggy BZZZZZness* chart on the other side. Fold the construction paper again to make a booklet. On the outside front cover, have students title this work and write their names.

DIAGNOSTIC NOTES

Look for students who:
  — understand and generate factual considerations.
  — apply their considerations to make valid choices.
  — support their points of view.
  — recognize other viewpoints.

Watch for a complexity of thought that demonstrates the capacity to see other points of view, which recognizes that weighing a variety of factors may be a never-ending process, and that addresses the importance of ecological interrelationships.

Name ____________________

A Very Buggy BZZZZZness

Wow! You can choose what bugs will live in your world! What bugs will there be? Why? What are your considerations?

BUGS	Yes	✓	No	✓
Black Ants				
Swallowtail Butterflies				
Ground Beetles				
House Flies				
Orb Weaver Spiders				
Honey Bees				
Dragonflies				
Crickets				
Ladybug Beetles				
Fireflies				

Name ________________________________

A Very Buggy BZZZZZness

Cut out the bugs you want in your world.

Glue them into your picture.

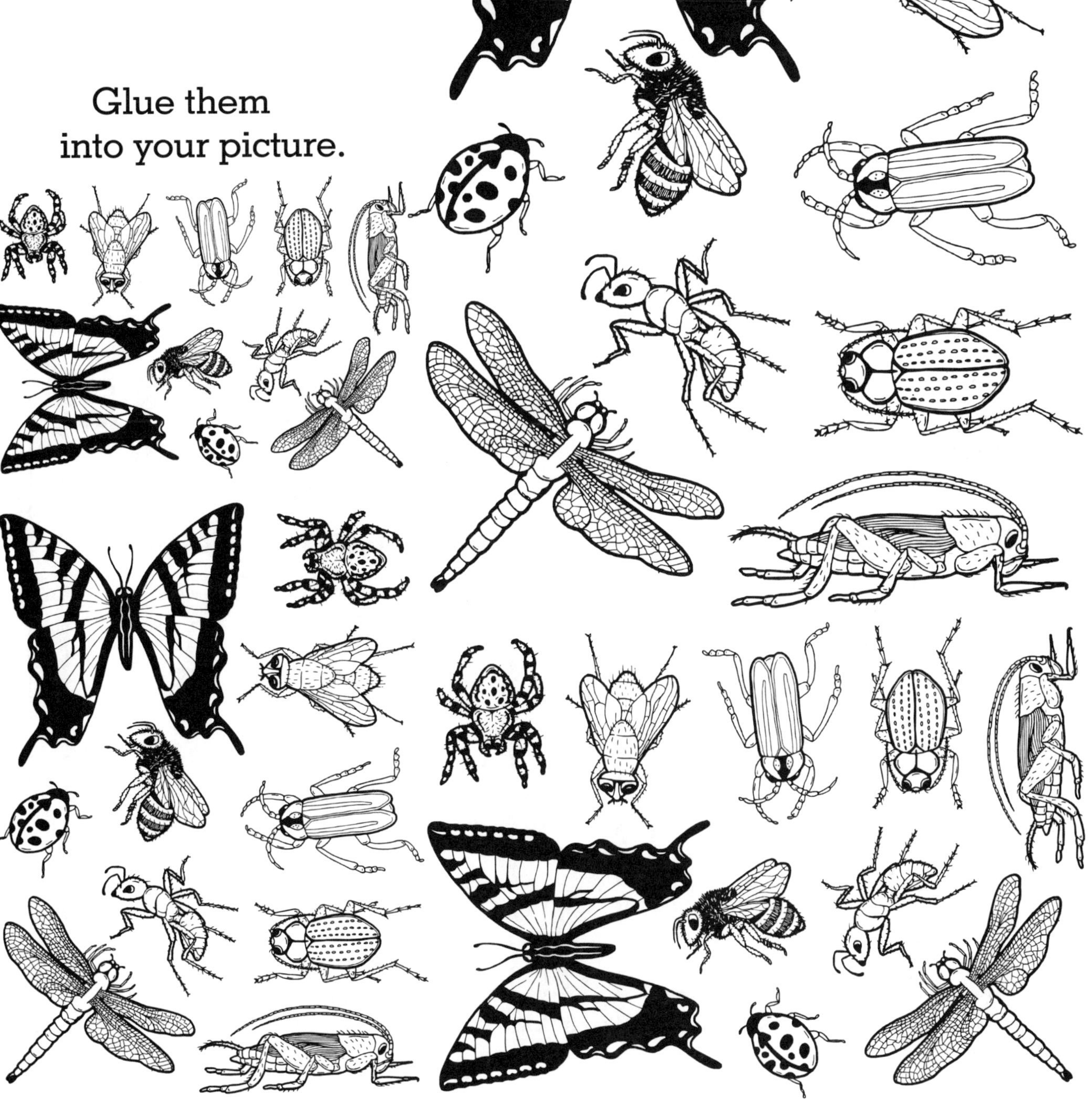

Ask me what I did
in
Thinking Skills
today!
. . . using considerations to find the best answer . . .

Ask me what I did
in
Thinking Skills
today!
. . . using considerations to find the best answer . . .

Ask me what I did
in
Thinking Skills
today!
. . . using considerations to find the best answer . . .

Ask me what I did
in
Thinking Skills
today!
. . . using considerations to find the best answer . . .

Convergent / Deductive Thinking

Divergent / Inventive Thinking

Notes

Convergent / Analytical Thinking

Divergent / Creative Thinking

Notes

Visual / Spatial Perception

Evaluative Thinking

Notes